MW01181285

BE THE ONE

Awakening a generation of difference makers.

Steven Sexton

Contact author at info@stevensexton.com
Visit him at stevensexton.com

ISBN 978-0-9794076-1-1

Book Formatting by Adam Jones
Contact at 501-624-1952

Contents

What They're Saying...

"This book is not only captivating, but life empowering. It issues a challenge to the reader to step up and answer the call on their life to *be the one.*"

Pastor Tim Brooks
Pastor of Christian Ministries Church
and Founder of Applied Life Ministries

"I'm convinced if every God-lover would look down on the inside of their heart, they would connect with the powerful truth revealed in these pages. It's a rallying call to all believers to stand up and fight for others."

Darian Rains
Senior Pastor at Your Place Church

"It's convicting, compelling, inspiring, and at the same time encouraging. I would recommend his book to every youth pastor as a resource for stirring up the hearts of your leaders and young people."

Jason Laird
Youth Pastor at Healing Place Church

"Everyone longs to make a difference, but often we lack the courage to "stand alone" and do what's right. This book will train you; reading it is only the beginning..."

Hettie Lue Brooks
Founder of Brookhill Ranch Summer Camp

"A timely, powerful message for a timely and powerful generation!"

Chris Chambers
Youth Pastor at Oasis Church

"Not only will youth be inspired, but as a youth minister for more than 14 years, I was challenged to *be the one* myself."

JD Buckridge
Sales & Promotions at New Life Radio

Introduction

Never before has our Christian culture been so poised and ready to do something great. I stand amazed as I see God reviving the heart of this generation. Hopefully you have felt the Holy Spirit stirring your heart to reach for more. More growth, more influence and more of his presence.

This generation is capable of producing the next great awakening. The Great Awakening was a time when God set off the alarm clock and the church woke up from a spiritual slumber. America broke out in a revival and the spiritual condition of the world was changed. Now we are again in need of another great move of God. We can't settle for great church services alone. Our mission is to have a great impact on this culture. This is our time. This is our moment. However, there are two schools of thought. The first is to wait and watch the events unfold, hoping that someone will emerge to answer the call. The second is for you to *be the one* and take the steps to influence your culture for Christ.

I know that last sentence was both uncomfortable and challenging. But the reality is we have lost something and we need to get it back. We have lost believers who are willing to pay the price and take action. Where are the men and women of God who will stand in the midst of great adversity to proclaim His message? It's insulting that God's people who know the answer have been unwilling to engage the lost. We've become captivated by our own selfish desires and have made our faith a hobby instead of a conviction. We stand in Christian meetings all over the world desiring God to serve us, while the mission God has called us to fulfill lies dormant. The sad part is, we've become a bunch of self-absorbed country club attendees rather than believers filled with faith, purpose, and the Holy Spirit.

I have written "Be the One" to awaken a generation of difference makers. My prayer is that the message in this book will serve as an alarm clock producing a loud piercing call to action. We can't sleep through or ignore the mandate Jesus has given to us. It was Jesus who told his disciples to go and influence the world with the message of truth. There is no snooze button when it comes to God's agenda. You can't tell Him, "I'll get to it later". Either you respond to the call or you don't.

By reading this book you will see that a partnership with God takes authentic faith. You can't have faith in yourself, your church, or your works; your faith must be a living, breathing, working faith. It must say, "God, if you are with me who can be against me?"

Many times God used a man or woman to speak to people, nations, and even the world. God chose King David to *be the one* to establish Israel for His purpose. David's desire was to worship and honor the Lord. Because of his devotion, he was willing to take on any giants that would stand against the one true God. David will be a key figure as we discover what it takes to embrace life's opportunities. My hope is that, as you read this book, you will allow God to speak directly to your heart so transformation can begin. This is not light reading; it's a Holy Spirit encounter designed to open blind eyes and cause clarity of purpose.

Who will hear the alarm and awake from their slumber? Now is the time to decide, do you want to stay comfortably nestled in the bed of self-importance and religious practices? Or will you roll back the blankets of apathy?

The assignment we've been given is undeniable. Don't wait any longer; God is ready for you to ***be the one.***

The One Needed

"Then He said to His disciples, 'The harvest is plentiful, but the workers are few.'"

Matthew 9:37

Can you hear that? It's silence. It's coming from what should be the loudest voice in the world, God's church. How could the Church, which has so much potential, be wrestling with a lack of influence in today's culture? Is it because the church is not needed anymore? No, that can't be, because the Bible clearly states that the gates of hell can't destroy the church. It also says Christ Jesus is coming back for His church. So why is the church fading? Why is the message of Christ becoming diluted with other **man-made** religions? In order to answer this question it will be a bit uncomfortable. Because God has not changed, and the devil hasn't either. So what has changed? US! Believers!

We've changed. No longer do we care about living the teachings of Christ. Instead we would rather listen to them and shake our heads in agreement. The church is on the verge of losing its influence because we would rather fight over doctrine than focus our attention on the real enemy. The problem is not the message of the church, but the people who come only to attend. We've become infatuated with our lives and our stuff. We have left no room for God's leading.

I believe there is a change coming. The stage is set for believers to make an impact that can save a generation. The alarm clock is going off, and it's screaming, "*Get up*!" No longer can the prompting of the Holy Spirit be disregarded. Awaken to the possibility that you are needed. **Awaken to the idea that God is looking for you to** *be the one* **who will proclaim His name.**

During the pages of this book, together we will uncover what it takes to be the one. I know that my style of writing is a bit in your face, but I'm not writing this to make you feel better about where you are. I'm writing this to encourage you to *wake up and not waste your life.* People need to see the transforming power of God. We can't make them believe but we can give testimony to who Jesus is. Only when we wake up can we bring in a harvest of souls, ready to make Jesus King.

do you care?

Imagine that you're watching a suspenseful movie. The music intensifies and the danger around the corner is so extreme that you don't want to look. With a hand over your face peeking through the gaps of your fingers you muster up the courage to watch the plot unfold. The dark character is set to terrorize another innocent family. The naive family is clueless to the intentions of their sinister adversary. They have no idea of the havoc that will be wreaked nor the destruction being planned. But somewhere in the movie there is always one person that figures out what's really going on and cares enough to help. Yes, it's a fight. It's hard. There's usually a crazy amount of running involved in this scene. This is where *the one* tries to save the innocent by unraveling the plan that was set to destroy a family.

There are countless movies that could fit this description. But let's consider why someone would be willing to face great obstacles and danger to save a life. Is it because they were bored and had nothing to do? Maybe it's just about the money. Or could it be because they CARE? There's a harvest just waiting to be gathered. However, it will take believers who care enough to forfeit their own personal agendas in order to see lives saved. Plain and simple, it's time for God's people to be the ones who care!

If we are going to make a real impact, then God's priorities shouldn't be optional. They should be of the utmost importance as we live to care about what He cares about. Believers have been playing sideline Christianity far too long, being happy to be on the team, but never really in the game. It's vital for us to get in the game and start a real relationship with Him. Then we can love what He loves and hate what He hates. He made it clear. He cares about being first in our lives and loving people.

Yeah I know, we care, but only to a point. We hate the violence, abortion, divorce rate, and all other vicious injustices in the world. But our caring is detached. It never goes past the initial feeling. There is rarely any action to our caring. What if in the movie example, the one who figured out the enemy's plan just thought to himself... "Wow, this is terrible! Someone should do something about this..." However, if the hero does nothing to help it would make for a lame movie. Similarly, your life is meant for something more—something that impacts people!

You can't turn on the television without seeing the need for young people to care and *be the one*. The only setback to unleashing this great move is that many believers find themselves full of compromise. King Saul found himself in this type of situation. His poor decisions cost him his influence and left the nation in need. Look carefully as we read about the removal of King Saul.

the one removed

King Saul was the first King of Israel, which was a huge deal. Why? Because God had been the King of Israel. He was the one to lead and govern them, but the people rejected God as their king. They wanted to be like the other cultures in the land and have a person as king. God honored their request and provided a man for them. So guess who was picked? That's right, Saul.

Everyone had high hopes for Saul. This guy was the total package. He was more impressive than Zac Efron's basketball skills (wink, wink). He was someone all of Israel could rally behind. Saul started out on top of his game! He won a few battles, but along the way he started compromising and then ultimately stopped caring about God's plan. His personal well-being became his focus, making it about him and not God. Does this sound familiar? Just like we mentioned earlier Saul was forfeiting his influence because he went to sleep spiritually. Many times the alarm went off; in fact there are three specific times where Saul could have heard the warning. But those warnings never really affected him. He forgot about the mission and made everything about him. He became consumed with his appearance, success, and people more than being the one.

Finally the time came when the prophet Samuel had to lay down the smack. It was a reality check that would rock any leader. Samuel told King Saul... *you're fired*! It was done with such authority that even Donald Trump would have taken notes. Let's look at the verse, 1 Samuel 15:27-28. It reads, "As Samuel turned to leave, Saul caught hold of the hem of his robe, and it tore. Samuel said to him, 'The Lord has torn the kingdom of Israel from you today and has given it to one of your neighbors, to one better than you." Samuel tells King Saul like it is. No fluff, no sugar coating, he tells him, "Because of your lack of obedience, you have lost the anointing and your position as king."[1]

There is no doubt Saul was given every opportunity to *be the one*. He was given: position, influence, favor, grace, and people to serve. Yet it all came to a screeching halt because Saul forgot his real purpose. It wasn't to be famous or to be a household name. He lost sight of where he was needed. He was needed to be a king who was obedient to God and a tool of blessing for God's people. **When we stop caring our actions will always remove us from influence.** Take a moment and ask yourself these questions, "How faithful am I being with His message? Are my decisions causing me to be removed from God's best?" Answering these questions will reveal how much you really care. Jesus said, "the harvest is ready but the laborers are few."[2] We are needed to bring in the harvest. However, **we can never reach our potential if we forfeit our opportunities.**

missed opportunities

Ouch! Imagine the sting of Samuel and Saul's convo. King Saul is feeling pretty good about himself, and then the hammer drops. Samuel tells him, "You're out big boy. Because you wouldn't listen, your rebellion to the Word of the Lord has cost you the kingdom. I wanted you to be the man, give God's message, and lead His people. Saul, you were His avenue of blessing, but you have missed your opportunity." (Paraphrased)

It's very sad when you see powerful men and women of God miss opportunities. People who had great influence and could have used their influence to rally a great movement of God. Yet because of broken focus, their influence was shattered before reaching its potential. I'm not judging anyone. My heart is to give mercy to any of the fallen who have repented. We all need mercy at one point or another for the decisions we've made. People do fall, and as hurtful as it is, we have to be ready to forgive and pick up where we left off.

What I find so fascinating about this story is that God had already chosen David to fill the gap. David was the go to-guy! God was in need of someone He could totally trust, and David was that man. Like a coach needing a player, God looked down at his bench and said, "Yes...David is ready. Get him in there!" How amazing would it be, to be God's gap filler? Here God comes to you and says, "I need you to complete a task that only you are equipped to do." How incredible! What you need to see is this life counts. Both Saul and David were given incredible opportunities to meet the need. One was blinded by pride and rebellion, the other was led by a heart after God. He's calling your name and saying, "*Get in there. You're needed*!"

Right before Jesus left the disciples He gave them a shout out that said, "Do what I've taught you and transform lives by making more disciples, baptizing them in the name of the Father, Son and Holy Spirit."[3]

This was a "must do" statement. As a parent, I have given many directive statements. My kids understand when dad gives a "must do," it must get done. A "must do" statement is a phrase that means this is not optional, debatable, or negotiable. Believers can easily forfeit their opportunity to change the world because they see God's mandates as optional. ***The conversation Jesus was having with the disciples about teaching others wasn't exclusively for them. Matt 29:18 was written for all believers.*** We can't have a "that's good for those people" mindset. This is a call to action. God needs you to respond accordingly and care.

He's looking for you

God is always looking for gap fillers, role players, and people who respond to the need. He wants you to be a role player in His plans. Ezekiel 22:30 says, "I looked for a man among them who would build up the wall and stand before me in the gap on behalf of the land so I would not have to destroy it, but I found none."[4] The Bible has scores of names of different people who said, "Yes, I'll *be the one*": Abraham, Noah, Gideon, Esther, Deborah, Peter, Mary, and Paul – to name just a few. Their names ring out in story after story, sermon after sermon, as people to this day give account of their commitment to God. The simple truth is they answered the call. They cared about Him, His people, and His plan. They made this commitment during some of the most crazy, wild, violent, no-chance-of-winning moments in time. The Bible says in Romans, "...If God be for us then who can be against us."[5] Meaning, by yourself you may be the minority, but with God you're the majority. So don't look at what you can or cannot do, look at what God can do through you. **God is looking for people who will have enough faith to dream big.** Don't stay confined to an average life. Think beyond your limitations. God loves it when you allow Him to love and care through you!

What I'm talking about is more than just humanitarian efforts. We have a world full of caring people. In America alone, we have "85 million households that give away money each year to nonprofit organizations."[6] However, what good is all the caring in the world if people don't get the answer that will ultimately save their lives? Is a warm meal more important than a soul saved from Hell? Is buying a red phone to help Africa what the Gospel message is all about? How about giving to the next big celebrity fundraiser? Is that being the one? NO!

Now, all of these ideas do make a difference in our world. They add some hope, friendliness, and are timely for those in need. But, the question I raise is: Does caring mean just meeting the physical needs and allowing the spiritual condition of a person to be neglected? I once heard that good is the worst enemy of best. God is looking for His people to refuse to be satisfied with just good living and nice gestures. God is looking for His people to go for the best, to give the full picture, the complete answer, and tell the whole truth.

What kind of help would we be to mankind if we left them fed, warm, and sheltered, but without truth? **If our caring doesn't lead the lost to a relationship with Him then we don't care enough.**

the need

You may be asking yourself, "Does God really need me? I mean come on. It's God. Can't He find someone else to do what He wants?" What we fail to understand is that God made us in His image with nothing lacking. In fact, He called us perfect and the Bible says that even the angels desire to do what we do.[7] For too long the devil has lied to generations by telling them they have no value and no significance. You were created to have dominion! You are no joke. Just look in Genesis 2 and see for yourself. God created mankind to be a difference-maker. You can *be the one* who communicates the Gospel message to this lost world. Yes, there is a need like never before in this culture to experience the transforming power of God. Will you be willing to meet the need?

There is a situation in the book of Esther where she decided to answer this question. The Jewish people were on the verge of being destroyed and Queen Esther had a decision to make. Would she *be the one* and come into the king's court unannounced? You didn't just walk up to a king who was conducting a meeting, especially if you were a woman. To interrupt the king could mean death. Would she help her people or sit back and do nothing? How big was her commitment to the Lord? How much did she really care? It's easy to say, "Someone should do something," but in this case, that someone was Esther. In our culture that someone is ***you***.

Look at what her cousin said in Esther 4:12-14: "Do not think that because you are in the king's house, you alone, out of all the Jews will escape. For if you remain silent at this time, relief and deliverance for the Jews will arise from another place, but you and your father's family will perish. And who knows but that you have come to royal position for such a time as this."[8]

Please understand there is no lack in God. He wins every time! The book of Revelation informs us that in no way is God up against the ropes, holding His hand out, waiting to tag up so we can get in there and fight. God has a time for everything and His Son, King Jesus, will reign and there is nothing the devil can do about it. It's going to happen. However, in every decade, with every culture, there is an opportunity for the *one* to emerge. Why? Because there is a need! When the darkness gets darker there is always a need for courageous people of God to fulfill their purposes and shine the light of truth. This generation is hurting and desperate for something that will last. These are not just words on a page. I believe the Spirit of God is stirring your heart to respond to the need.

This type of caring is not something you can do by yourself. It's supernatural. This type of caring is fueled by the Holy Spirit. God is the only one who can provide a love that looks past the stain of sin in order to connect with the sinner. We are too critical, judgmental, and fault-finding to really love the people who are in need. This is why it's so important for God to be the love you can't be in the flesh. We must allow Him to love through us.

the time is now

The moment has come for us to put away the mindset of just waiting for God. We must start being the people in whom God can do something. *We can make a difference.* God has given us all the ability to choose what kind of impact we will have on our family, friends, and community. To be inactive is no longer a viable option.

Just turn on the news; open your eyes. The need is overwhelming. The world is looking for leadership. They are sick and tired of the lies, betrayal, and lack of character coming from today's leaders. The time is now for you to start preparing your heart and mind. This generation must desire influence so we can share Him. No longer can we afford to be silent. ***Our words and actions should prove to the world that we will not fade into the background.***

Who will care enough about the spiritual condition of our culture to do something about it? The generation before us will be judged by what they have allowed, and so will we. There is no doubt David was a difference maker. God didn't just randomly pick David. David had obviously picked God and made the choice to open his heart and submit his life.

During the next few chapters, we will take a closer look at David's life as he says yes to God and the destiny for his life.

David embodies the concept of the one by caring enough to take action, and most importantly, giving his heart to the Lord. The people of Israel wanted a king. But no matter how impressive he was physically, Saul was missing something internally. There was a need in the kingdom and God had already made His choice. David would *be the one* to make a difference and lead God's people into all that He had for them. I believe you will do the same. Lets get started!

The One Chosen

"The eyes of the Lord search the whole earth in order to strengthen those whose hearts are fully committed to Him."
2 Chronicles 16:9 NLT

God is committed to raising up a generation of Christian leaders who will speak of Him. His eyes are continually searching for the few who are ready to make a difference, yet for the ones to emerge, it's essential that they leave behind their thoughts of insignificance. God has chosen you to be a part of His great plan. Just think how awesome it is that God would partner with us. We get the opportunity to carry His transforming message to the world. Yet many times believers feel too insignificant to embrace the concept that God has chosen them.

Do you ever feel too average to do something big? Do you ever get discouraged because you feel inadequate to fulfill your dreams? There are a number of young people I have worked with who doubted their significance. They have bought into the lie that nothing substantial can come from them. I'm so glad King David didn't think this way while Samuel was anointing him as the next king of Israel. He could have thought, "I'm nothing like my brothers." or "What good can come from being a shepherd?" It seems like many believers in our society are content to live average, ordinary lives. They're okay with going to work and doing church occasionally. They only live to be entertained. However, we serve a supernatural God who is merely waiting for someone to say, *"I don't want to be average.* I'll pay the price. Whatever it costs, God, I'll *be the one!"*

why david?

With just a little reading from the Bible we can see that the hand of God was on David's life. But let's ask the question: What were David's qualifications to be king? Was it because David was a good kid and didn't fight with his brothers? Or maybe it was because of David's excellent shepherding skills. Was David chosen for his musical talents? Maybe he was the only teenager at this time who cleaned his room. Did God randomly pick him? Or was there something significant about the choice God made? David certainly had something that the previous king had lost. In fact, God tells us about the difference in 1 Samuel 16:7. It says:

"But the Lord said to Samuel, 'Do not look at his appearance or at his physical stature, because I have refused him. For the Lord doesn't see as man sees; for man looks at the outward appearance, but the Lord looks at the heart.'" [1]

I love this verse because it is evident that God is educating Samuel. God is showing him how He chooses the one. Can you imagine being there? King Saul was just told that the anointing on him was over. Then Samuel goes off to pick another king. While Samuel is processing who will be the next king, Eliab walks in. Dude is a monster. Samuel is immediately impressed. Surely he's the new king…right? But God stops him and says, "Hey bro, don't pick on first impressions. The guy I have in mind has something different, something special. I'm looking at what he's got going on in his heart and it's impressive. So don't pick prematurely. Wait and I will show you the one." Wow! God is arranging a meeting for David that he didn't even know about. God was sending a prophet because He noticed what David already had inside and liked it. **What meeting, advancement, or opportunity is God working on now that you don't even know about?** David was chosen because of the condition of his heart. Is your heart getting the attention of God?

one right heart

For David, it was his heart that brought the favor of God upon him. Yet he wasn't perfect by any means. There were many moments of compromise and downright evil actions. However, God—knowing the end from the beginning—still chose David to *be the one*. Both Saul and David were chosen by God to lead the people. They were both skilled and capable. However, Saul was removed and David was established. What was the difference between them? The real difference was their hearts. **The motives of a person's heart are always revealed by adversity and inspection.** These men had very different responses when it came to correction. When Saul made a wrong decision, he was sorry he got caught and gave excuses. When David's sins were exposed, he repented because he knew he had grieved the Lord. Can you see the difference between the two king's hearts? It's so easy to make excuses instead of repenting. This generation is so good at justifying their position. They go to great efforts to try and save themselves from painful consequences. In doing so, they do themselves more harm than good. Their heart becomes hardened and unable to hear truth that can set them free!

God's heart for you is huge! This is why He sent Jesus, His Son, to die for you. His sacrifice provided freedom from sin. This revelation of sacrifice revives your heart so that He can connect with you. Why? God is not satisfied with just a portion of your heart. He is looking to fill it completely.

What you allow in your heart is so important because God will advance the one with a right heart. It's no surprise that shepherds and kings don't mix. The goal of a shepherd wasn't to be king. The only way to be king was through the bloodline. The best a shepherd could do was be a shepherd. For David, it didn't matter where he started because his heart was going to take him further than his birthright, his talents, or his IQ. His heart was free from excuses and arrogance. The Word of God was in David's heart and he had a desire to please the Lord.

What you allow to develop in your heart will determine the road you travel in life. The person who has a heart full of pride, rebellion, and compromise will never be used to his or her full potential. God wants His chosen people to live a life that is set apart. The world's ideologies should not usurp the calling of God on your life. I'm very aware that temptations are all around us. They pull and persuade people to make the wrong choices. To be effective it's vital that we learn how to fight our flesh and protect our hearts from becoming hard, rebellious, and numb. I'm not saying those who have a right heart will never blow it or make the wrong choices. We all have to deal with missing the mark and sinning. When this happens, we repent and return to God's way of living. When we don't, we put our hearts and relationship with God in real danger.

Remember the heart of a person is identified by their responses. You can't hide what is operating in your heart. Because when pressure is applied, who you really are will always come out. As we continue to read about David, it's clear that when pressure was applied in his life, he always turned to the Lord. This is why David was chosen. His heart was after God. Look at the condition of your heart. When adversity hits you, who do you turn to? Is the cry of your heart to know God or does He just get an honorable mention in your life?

Imagine you have a large pizza that is cut into eight slices. Those slices can be given to anyone you want. In the same way, your heart can be easily divided and given away. That's why who you give your heart to is so important. David had many responsiblities but his heart was totally given to God. Our God is not satisfied with a divided heart. He wants it all! Just because you go to church doesn't mean He has been allowed to capture your heart. To *be the one*, allow Him to captivate your attention. Only then will you begin to lay down those areas that compete against God for your attention. Only then will you begin to lay down pride, selfishness, and rebellion. When you can willingly say, "God, I choose you," that is when you become someone who is operating in a right heart.

whose choice is it?

Probably the greatest feeling in the world is the one of being chosen. I remember when I was in fourth grade and we would meet every day to play football. As soon as recess began, we were off to the field and the fifth graders would start to pick teams. I learned ever so quickly that there were some requirements for being chosen... like being good. If the fifth graders didn't think you could catch, block, or defend then you were reduced to a spectator. Every time they started picking I'd get nervous. I wasn't the best player, but I wasn't terrible either. I was just average, but I still wanted to play. Everything in me was screaming "PICK ME!"

Now as I look back, I can see this event from a different perspective. You can learn a lot from playing football on the playground. There are no bailouts, tolerance, or affirmative action. The best contributors played. The questions I had to ask myself were, what was I doing to be in the game and how was I developing?

Many people are asking God to "pick me" so they can do something great. Yet they sit back and just dream, wanting God to do everything for them. The sad part about this is when the dream doesn't work out they begin to blame God, because He didn't do it. God is so faithful and any work that He begins will happen. But it will also take your effort, resources, and ability. Listen, **we don't work for God's love, but our work shows God how much we love Him.** The greatness of a person's impact is determined by their daily effort. God will open the door, but we have to walk through it.

Please understand, God loves you and has desired to know you from the beginning. He doesn't think of you as average; in fact, He thinks you're "fearfully and wonderfully made."[2] As far as He is concerned, you are already chosen. He sent His Son, Jesus, to pick you and put you on the team. God wants you in the game, but the choice is yours. There is a specific assignment for your life. You have been called to *be the one*.

the answer God wants to hear

As a parent, some of the greatest moments in child rearing are when your kids come up to you and say, "I love you." But more than that is when my children respond to the instruction I give them with joy, urgency, and efficiency. It's during those times that they are putting the phrase "I love you" into action and showing me their love. Too many times in our relationship with God, we express the phrase but not the actions. It's hard to show your love for the Lord if your actions don't line up with your words. There is a real choice to make and the answer God longs to hear is "Yes, I'll do whatever it takes."

Consider Mary, the mother of Jesus. She was engaged to Joseph, an engagement which was intended to last a year. There was to be no hanky panky, if you know what I mean. The culture of that day placed great importance on honor, character, and commitment. Mary was a virgin and she needed to stay that way until after the wedding ceremony.

Then the angel of the Lord came to Mary and said, "You're going to have a baby."[3] Let's just think about this for a while. Can you imagine what a huge responsibility this would be, being the mother of the Son of God? Mary had never been a mother before. What qualification did she have to mother the King of Kings and Lord of Lords? This takes babysitting to a whole notha level. Yet, the Bible says that she was highly favored by God.[4]

This story usually gets attention at Christmas time as we are honoring the birth of our Savior, but just for a second, stop and really think about this: Mary was face to face with a *be the one* moment. Would she back down? What about Joseph? How would she explain her pregnancy? Would people really believe this was the Lord? However, all of these thoughts were silenced when she answered the angel, "Yes, I'll do it just like you say."[5] You see, God clearly chose Mary, but that's not the end of the story. Mary had to choose to follow God's plan and do it exactly as He said. Because of Mary's answer, she was chosen to birth the greatest gift mankind has ever known.

the correct response

So far we've covered many characters. Each character's response either removed the influence they had or moved them into more influence. Saul's anointing to be king was taken from him because of his wrong responses. David, Esther, and Mary all came into what God had for them because they chose the right response. It's true, the choice is yours and you can make whatever decision you want to make. However, **the heart that pleases God is the one with the correct response.** When David was chosen, it had nothing to do with his outward appearance, musical talent, or even his bravery; David's road to influence started with his heart.

Countless times the Bible records how God's chosen people responded wrongly to His leading. In fact, the children of Israel were saved, led out of Egypt, had provision for every need, and still came up with numerous wrong responses. Numbers 13 tells us the story of the Lord telling Moses to send out twelve spies to check out the land He was giving them. The men were gone forty days and when they came back to give their report to Moses it was full of negativity. They basically said, "Moses, we can't go against these people. We will get beat down. These guys are huge!"[6]

Because of their response, the generation that could have taken the land died in the wilderness instead. This can happen to us as well. As a culture, we could settle for the wilderness and never accomplish the mission. Are you settling for the wilderness, never really getting to the Promised Land? Your responses are what position you to receive more. Israel was still God's chosen people, but because they made the wrong choice many never got to experience the promise land.

Every day we have to respond to obstacles in our lives. Those who learn to respond right experience more fulfillment. **The one who provides the right response in crucial moments tends to avoid major setbacks.** How are your responses with your family and authorities? How would the people in your life describe the way you handle setbacks and pressures? Do you quit when your plans aren't going as expected? Do you get mad and offended when people question you?

Our man David wasn't even invited to the meeting with Samuel. They had to go and get him because David's own father didn't even consider him. Just think how David could have responded when they showed up to get him from the flock. He could have said, "What...now you want me to come? I've been with the sheep while my brothers got to go to a special meeting with Samuel and now you come get me? No way, not me! I have way too much respect and dignity to be the last one who comes before Samuel. You tell him, I'm not interested!" This would be the typical response from our culture. But, this is not the response God would have us give. When disappointment comes, God wants us to respond with faith and courage. So don't throw away opportunities by being easily offended.

To *be the one*, make the decision to elevate your responses from flesh to faith. God has chosen you to make a difference in our world. You have to allow Him to transform your life. **Stop waiting on God, because more often than not, God is waiting on you.**

guidelines for the chosen

To live a life that brings God glory it takes more than just a quick decision at the altar. David's influence wasn't based on his verbal commitment to the Lord. It went much deeper than that. David responded to the assignments God gave him with faith, obedience, humility, and courage. There was action behind David's success. To see God bring you to a level of influence, these virtues are not optional. Let's spend some time on these.

1. *Faith-* **nothing can happen in a believer's life without faith.** In fact, the Bible says, "Without faith it is impossible to please Him, for he who comes to God must believe that He is, and that He is a rewarder of those who diligently seek Him".[7] I believe one of the reasons we have not seen the great works of God in our generation is because we don't believe He'll do it. We know He can. We know He has in the past. But we lack the faith that is ready to believe *big*. No longer can we settle for weak faith. God wants you to believe Him. Don't live a powerless life. Remember you are chosen! There is more! Let's stop forfeiting our defining moments because of a lack of faith. Nothing is too big for God! Our part is to have faith and give God the avenue to move, heal, and transform.

Time and time again we see David as a man of faith. He believed not only that God could, but he also had confidence that God would stand behind His Word. As a result, David's life was full of extraordinary stories of God's faithfulness.

2. *Obedience-* God demands that His chosen be obedient. We know He loves the sinner, the rebellious, and even the wicked, but it's the obedient He will trust with deep revelation. Where there is no mandate for obedience, mayhem is sure to follow. It's the obedient who take the Word of God and the promptings of the Holy Spirit and act. Jesus said in John 14:15, "If you love me, you will obey what I command."[8] You can't have a deep relationship with Jesus and disregard His words.

Sure there is grace, and I'm so grateful when I fall short that God doesn't disown me or strike me with lightning. Instead, He brings conviction and correction to me when I'm starting to get off-course. Why? Because God never ignores our sins. For those who choose to obey, influence is sure to follow. God is not demanding perfection; He just wants your heart. Do you have a sincere desire to honor Him as the Lord of your life?

What action does God want to ignite in your life? Has fear or pride kept you inactive? **Obedience is not always comfortable, but without it we never leave the category of potential.** It's time for God's people to move from potential to production. I believe in my spirit that God wants to turn a rebellious generation into obedient producers for Him. Let's change the world!

3. *Humility*- it would be foolish for us to believe that everything hinges on us. The Bible says, "for promotion comes neither from east, from west, nor from south but from Him."[9] Humility removes the temptation to be self-sufficient, and it reminds us that we need the Lord. God doesn't give us favor, position, and advancement so we can forget Him. He provides that level of influence so we can promote Him.

The absence of humility will destroy the longevity of a producer. Everything you've been given is for you to steward, not to own. Your talents and intellect should lead you to your knees in thankfulness, not puff up your pride.

It's so funny to me that we can be so prideful when it comes to our talents. Lebron James doesn't get to pick his height, athletic ability, or speed. Carrie Underwood doesn't get to pick her vocal range. We cheer for a 6'8" basketball star that has an arm reach of 3 feet and are amazed when he can dunk a basketball when the rim is only 10 feet high. Now let me ask you, did he have anything to do with that? I'm not dogging Lebron. I'm a huge fan. I love watching basketball. It just amazes me how easily pride can develop over something which we have no control. Yes, the singer and athlete have some choices to make. They can practice. They make the most of their talent and opportunities. There are many choices that can advance your influence, but pride is a destroyer. The Bible says, "He scorns the scornful, but gives grace to the humble."[10] It's only when we humble ourselves before the Lord that we get to continue travelling down the path He has set before us. Remember, all of your talents are given so you can promote Him.

4. *Courage*- **many believers stop short of experiencing great moves of God because they lack the courage to step out and believe the impossible.** It's like the motto of our Christian culture is, "Don't attempt anything you can't do." That's ridiculous. What if Moses, the one chosen to deliver God's people out of Egypt, didn't have the courage to stretch the staff over the water of the Red Sea? What if Joshua didn't believe that God could use him to take the land of Canaan? What if David looked at the 9 foot tall warrior, Goliath, and said, "I don't blame you guys. I wouldn't want to fight him either." I write all of these examples from the Bible to show

you that it was average, ordinary people who God used to do extraordinary things. The one element they all have in common was courage! Maybe they didn't start out that way, but they all became believers; not in their abilities but in God's.

The stench of apathy has overcome the body of Christ. We have become weak, intimidated believers who cling to the walls of the church rather than bringing His church to break down the walls in people's lives. It says in the Bible, "If God be for me then who can be against me?"[11] As you're reading this book, I pray that the boldness of Christ would empower you to tell others about the greatness of God. You are the one! Not the silent ones, not the "I–will–when–I–understand–more" ones. The courage to act is rooted and grounded in Christ. It can save a life, start a movement, and change a culture if you will just be the one to act.

more than a choice

God has chosen you, but that is not enough. Now it's your choice. Leave everything else behind and transform your thoughts to be like Christ. Only then will you emerge as the one! It's no accident you're reading this book. I believe the Spirit of God is stirring something so deep in you that it will ignite who God has made you to be. However, it's more than a choice, it's a lifestyle of choosing. Everyday life brings us choices we have to make. But understand, none are bigger than choosing Him.

The One Who Is Ready

"Get yourself ready! Stand up and say to them whatever I command you."

Jeremiah 1:17

I love going on vacation with my family. Of course, with six of us there are countless decisions that need to be made. There are calendars to check, a destination to choose, bags to pack, and what route to take. All of this must be done before we leave in order to make the most of our time together. Although preparation plays a huge part in planning a trip, it is also vital to every area of life. It is not enough to want to make a difference. We need to be ready when the time comes. Without preparation, time is wasted, and opportunities fall short.

We are called to make a difference in this generation. Jesus said we are to be a light, like a city on a hill.[1] This means we stand out. Not to draw attention to ourselves, but to the transforming work that's Jesus has done. The Christian life is a beacon of light that projects the message, "Look at Him." Don't hide this message. Be ready to do your part by preparing now. There is no doubt in my mind that you're meant for more but to accomplish it you'll have to be ready when the time comes.

the importance of preparation

Preparation starts the process of seeing your dreams and potential fulfilled. Having a dream is the easy part, but fulfilling the dream is totally different. Dreams don't just happen. **It's only when we're faithful and prepared that we prove ourselves capable of great things.** Too many times we procrastinate and put off the very areas of life we should be developing. These neglected areas have caused many believers to be ineffective, not ready to pursue the plan God has for them. David proved his faithfulness by how he submitted to the calling on his life. Would he be ready when the time came? In 1 Samuel 16:17-19, we see David's first opportunity to increase his influence.

> "So Saul said to his servants, 'Provide me now a man who can play well and bring him to me.' Then one of the servants answered and said, 'Look, I have seen a son of Jesse, the Bethlehemite, *who is skillful in playing, a mighty man of valor, a man of war, prudent in speech* and a handsome person; and the Lord is with him.' Therefore, Saul sent messengers to Jesse and said, 'Send me your son, David, who is with the sheep.'"[1] (emphasis added)

I know you just read this, but pay close attention to the part in italics. Can you believe the servants are talking about David? They describe him as talented, mighty, tough, and wise. It's like he was given an extreme makeover! This kid was a nobody when he met Samuel. If David represented these qualities Jesse would have made sure he was at the meeting with Samuel. Nothing is said about David having those attributes. Something happened! A change was made after David received the anointing. I believe David became focused and ready which ultimately put him in a situation to increase his influence.

Today God is saying, 'ready yourself.' Stop the wishful thinking that removes personal responsibility and start living everyday like it's important. To be ready for what God has is going to require more than just the willingness to act. Being ready means you have taken the necessary steps to ensure success. So when your moment comes, your action will be seasoned with maturity and stability. Only God can bring increase to a person's life. But if we fail to manage what He gives us, then influence will always be absent. God anointed David to be king, but there had to be a process of preparation before David knew how to be a king. Our goal is to be ready in every stage so that we don't limit what God has for us.

start the process

To start the process take an inventory of all God has given to you. Remember nothing is too small. Refuse to be satisfied with unmanaged gifts. There is always more. **In God's economy, more only comes to those who effectively manage their little.** When David started he didn't have a huge following, an impressive kingdom, or even a notable reputation. But he did have sheep and a harp. To some, this may look like nothing, but to God it was the beginning of more. It was how God would build His king. Committing to *be the one* is more than just slogans and statements. It's about people who will pay the price and start the process! Remember, Samuel anointed David's head with oil and the Spirit of the Lord came upon him. However, what happened next? Nothing! There was no announcement to the people, no parade honoring God's selection. The next event in David's life was going back to the sheep. How extremely frustrating is that? To be appointed to a new job, but have to stay at the old one.

Once David was anointed as king, he had only two options: just sit back and dream about his future or start working with what he had. Are you managing what you have? For example, your education, time, and money? Do you see the areas that can be developed? Are you ready to give yourself fully to the development of the gifts God has given you?

Many of you have dreams and desires. Maybe you want to be a writer, singer, pastor, teacher, professional athlete, business owner, etc. In order to see your dreams manifested, it will take a very unpopular word called *work*. There is no way David would have been instantly ready for the throne after his encounter with Samuel. Accomplishing all that God had for him would take time, effort, failure, growth, and personal investment. You're too valuable to the kingdom of God to just be a dreamer. Dreams aren't bad, in fact, they can be a catalyst for those willing to take the needed steps. Start working hard today to accomplish your dreams and goals. Don't worry about how everything will play out, just begin to take the steps to work the dream. The Bible often talks about God rewarding those who are faithful with what they have been given. Don't let your gifts lay dormant. With the right heart, God will bless whatever you manage. There will always be an increase for His faithful ones.

what's in your hand?

I've been in full-time ministry since 1999 and all of the areas that really produce for me started in my early teenage years. As a teenager, I loved:

- Talking (got in tons of trouble for it though)
- Children (had more fun in children's church than the children did)
- Music (played the drums in high school and had a rap group called God's Posse, but I don't really want to talk about it)
- Church (they had to lock me out, because I was always there)
- Leading (can you say overly excited?)
- Being the center of attention (see me, notice me, tell me that you love me)

Today, I'm using every one of these areas for the Kingdom of God. If you will develop what is in your hand, then I promise it will produce. In Psalm 37:4, it says that God will give you the desires of your heart.[2] All He requires is that you worship Him with what you have. Let's look again at 1 Samuel 16:17-18 very closely.

"So Saul said to his servants, 'Provide me now a man who can play well and bring him to me.' Then one of the servants answered and said "Look, I have seen a son of Jesse a Bethlehemite, who is skillful in playing, a mighty man of valor, a man of war, prudent in speech and a handsome person: and the Lord is with him."[3] David's sheep and harp were more than just occupation and entertainment. They were a part of his worship and development. David took care of those sheep as unto the Lord. Because of that, David's time was never wasted. His leadership was forged in the pasture and perfected on the throne. **What you have may seem like a little, but it is the start of something incredible.** Consider the trip we mentioned earlier. To get where we want to go we must be prepared. We must be ready!

The difference between Saul and David is that God picked Saul, but He got to build David. David entered a partnership with God. He wasn't using God to promote his agenda. He was allowing God to make him. Just like the potter and the clay work together to form something beautiful and useful. David had surrendered his life to *be the one*. Are you allowing God to mold you into someone with the capacity for great impact? It should be our hearts cry to ask the Master Builder to go to work in our hearts. To change our lives. Only then will we be useful. Only then will we have a life that is beautiful. What can you do today that can get you ready for God's next assignment? David's road to the kingdom wasn't based on an extraordinary résumé. It came through what he already had, a harp.

it's just a harp

David could've been another August Rush with the harp. Maybe the first time his fingers hit the strings he started rocking the music. However, if he was anything like the musicians I know, there were a lot of sore fingers, wrong notes, and endless practice. David had no idea that a harp would take him to the palace. Listen, God can use the most unlikely area of your life to promote you. David could have thought, "It's just a harp. I don't want to practice today." Or maybe there was a time when David decided to play a song for his family and they laughed. I'm sure there were times when he felt his songs weren't good enough. But the thing I want you to see is that doors were opening for David because he developed his gift.

What are the areas you excel in? It's time to start putting value on them. Stop comparing yourself to everyone else and start getting ready. Please understand there are no shadows in the kingdom of God. Meaning, God is not comparing you to anyone else. There have been plenty of great men and women who have served God mightily. Yet He doesn't rate you on a scale of better and worse. Because the same power that worked through them lives in you. The plan He has for you is specific and it will involve your gifts, talents, and efforts.

There is no denying, God will always bless what you use to bless Him. David developed the ability to play the harp to praise God. In psalm after psalm, David would write to his God, revealing the innermost parts of his heart. This was not just a hobby. When David played his harp you could hear his anthem. As he committed to work with what he had, his skill grew. This provided the anointing that was on him to finally have an outlet.

effort required

Not everything you do starts out great. There's a learning curve no matter what it is. From potty training to driving a car or playing a sport to becoming a parent, there's always something to learn. You may have the potential to be great in one area or another, but *potential without practice makes an underachiever.* Even if you're extremely gifted and can learn with ease, effort should still be given.

In 1971, a movie came out and was remade in 2005, called, "Willie Wonka and the Chocolate Factory."[4] In this movie, golden tickets were placed in chocolate candy bars. Anyone who found them got a trip to Willie Wonka's factory. (and a lot of chocolate) No skill was involved. It was just a random chance. Yet even with this chance of receiving a golden ticket, there was still effort. Someone had to work to buy the chocolate. They had to go to the store to get the chocolate. And they had to un-wrap the chocolate to see if the "golden ticket" was inside. Plus, we can't leave out the Oompa-Loompas who had to clean up all the messes.

Our society is becoming more and more of an entitlement society. It's like we've come under the illusion that we are owed something from someone or some system. I'm sorry, but this is not how life works. Focused, goal-oriented effort is what separates the achievers from the underachievers. How can the Body of Christ step into leading the church and our culture without personal effort? Maybe we are waiting for our golden tickets. Like Charlie, whose hope was solely in the golden ticket our hope is not in our effort but in God, the multiplier of effort. God has equipped you to speak a message that could change the world. To influence this generation, don't wait for a golden ticket. Take the necessary steps to make a real impact.

As believers, we see the gifts God has given to us different than the world. The world sees their gifts and talents as a way to promote themselves. But we see our gifts as a way to promote Him. **What God has blessed you with will provide help for others if you develop it.** The day is upon us when our friends, neighbors, and co-workers will be looking for answers. We can only give them what we have taken the time and effort to produce. They will be crying out just like King Saul. Those who choose to be the one and say, "I'm investing my efforts to see others receive healing, power and truth," will be the real difference makers in our culture.

There is more to this chapter than just a message of self-improvement. It's about caring enough to know the answer and the willingness to give it. This means we study the Word, know what we believe, live by it, and effectively communicate it. We cannot punk out and avoid the questions of a broken culture. It's easy to hide behind a fast paced life with an over-demanding schedule. Your generation is asking for the answer. Jesus Christ is that answer. He was sent to heal the broken. There is an anointing that comes when we speak about Him. The anointing that was on David's life caused his music to soothe the restlessness in Saul. In the same way, Jesus is the one that can soothe the restlessness in our culture. We cannot have peace by making more money. Peace doesn't come by being in a relationship, having a notable career or removing all the weapons of mass destruction. It only comes when we yield our lives and come under His Lordship.

There are instances when your efforts will be tested. Being tested is not negative. Without a driving test just imagine who would be on the road. Do you want a doctor to perform surgery on you if they never passed their medical test? A test is given to determine what you know. You can't move to new levels without passing the test. You are more than able to complete the assignment God has for you. Work hard and get your "A". In fact, the Bible says, "God will not put more on you than you can handle."[5] Every situation you are in right now is preparing you to *be the one*. Work hard and give your best effort. **Those who use their time for preparation will have a voice that influences others.** David was ready for the many tests that came because in his waiting he never rested!

use it or lose it

In Matthew 25:14-30, Jesus tells the story of a master who calls his servants together. The master says, "Hey guys! I'm about to bust out. I need to take care of some business. I'm leaving some money with you so you guys can continue the work on my project. The money is broken down based on your ability; I'll be back as soon as I can. You guys get busy!"[6]

Now in the scripture, the money that was distributed was called a talent (a unit of weight). This was no small amount of money. One talent was equal to 75.6 US pounds (of gold). Meaning based on today's market, one talent was about 1,504,742 dollars and some change. Wow! Can you say M-O-N-E-Y. Anyway, one servant was given five talents, another two, and the last one received only one talent. Can you imagine someone coming up to you and handing you over a million dollars and saying, "Hold this for me. I'll be back." After some time the master returned and was like, "Show me the money." The big boss man was wanting to see some return. It was time to inspect their effort. What had they been doing? Two of them were ready, because their effort had proven it. They had multiplied what they were given. But the servant who only received one talent did nothing! He didn't increase what he had. In fact, he took the talent and buried it. (Like that was a good idea! Who puts a million in the ground?) In disgust, the master took the talent away and called him lazy and wicked. The master got so mad he kicked him out of the house. Then, he gave the money that was in the ground to the one who had the most.

In this story the master is Jesus and He is coming again. There will be an inspection of heart, effort, and work. Remember, we don't work for salvation, but our work represents how much we value our salvation. The church can't be a country club of believers who, because of their membership, feel like no effort is required. We all have a part to play and this requires work. It is work to overcome your flesh by walking in the spirit. I don't love people because I'm a pastor; I love people because I'm a Christian. I don't give because I go to church; I give because God gave to me. I'm not trying to be good by following some religious system; my goal is to be like Him. All of this takes effort. It doesn't matter how much you've been given; what matters is what you do with it. Don't bury what God has given you. This world needs you!

The master gave the talents hoping the servants would increase what they had. He wasn't trying to catch them doing something wrong. God is not an over-demanding boss who is just waiting for you to mess up. He is a loving God who wants a real relationship with you. God wants to give you the opportunity to affect people's lives. Will you invest it in others or bury it?

When God makes an investment in you, it is because He knows you are able to do something with it. The real question comes down to your "want to." God has entrusted something great to you. So excuses will not work. Stop comparing your talents with everyone else's. God's only request is that you're faithful with what He has given you. The ball is in your court. Don't allow selfishness, fear of failure, or a lack of understanding, to keep your talent undeveloped. When you don't value and protect what He has given you, then you will lose opportunities to build His kingdom. There are so many ways to invest your gifts. Do something that shows that you are a producer, that you care, and that you're ready to *be the one*!

who's ready?

Sometimes it seems that when we start pursuing God's plan for our lives we get frustrated. We feel like it's not happening fast enough. However, God's ways don't always fit our timetable, but they are definitely sure. From the moment David was anointed to the taking of the throne, we can see the process of his preparation.

You see, God was giving David time to develop and mature. And when the time came, David was ready. Don't wait another day; start preparing what you have. There is nothing more fulfilling or exciting than allowing God to use you. As you commit to follow Him it will open up new opportunities and seasons of growth in your life. Now is the time to give your best and prepare the talents you've been given. Only then will influence come. This is why it is so important not to get side-tracked with areas that won't produce anything for the Kingdom of God. God has more for you, but it will only come if you decide to be ready.

The One To Embrace The Moment

"The Lord himself goes before you and will be with you; he will never leave you nor forsake you. Do not be afraid; do not be discouraged."

Deuteronomy 31:8

I believe God is about to release a gathering of committed Halo-type Christians who are poised and ready to *be the one*. Not to take this culture by force and start blowing up everything, but to show the devil that we are compelled to engage every giant that would try to keep us silent, scared, and subdued.

Like a soldier who fights for freedom, this generation of believers will not sit back and just hope for the best. This movement will be pioneered by those who embrace the moment instead of running from it. God has arranged incredible opportunities for the ones who are brave enough to meet their giants and not retreat. We see this kind of resolve in David as he was unwilling to be intimidated and give ground to Goliath.

No single battle has received as much attention as the epic battle of David and Goliath. Maybe you've heard about the nine foot Philistine giant who frightened the army of Israel so badly that they were reluctant to fight. How sad it is that Israel, God's chosen people, allowed their faith to be stolen. For forty days Goliath brought a challenge before God's people and they did nothing, because they were too scared to go on the offensive. What were they thinking? Didn't they remember whooping the Philistines when Saul was first anointed as king? Had they forgotten whose children they were? Countless times God had provided supernaturally for them. Yet here they stood backed up at the Valley of Elah, stagnant and unproductive, with Goliath shouting insults at them.

adversity reveals the one

It's only out of adversity that the one emerges. As we uncover what it takes to *be the one*, know that the one is validated when they re-think the situation and stay focused in the midst of critics. Only then can we embrace our moments with confidence and clarity. There's something in us all that loves to hear when someone beats the odds and wins. But odds aren't beaten by lucky breaks. It takes discipline, focus, and the assurance that God will give you what you need. That's why it's so important to have the correct perspective about life and its challenges. **Every decision you make comes from the seed of your thoughts.** The adversity Israel was up against caused them to need David. Yet David's outlook was not swayed by problems or other people. Like David, let's learn to see adversity as an opportunity to go to another level. There's no doubt about it, life is hard and there can be many setbacks, but when you know who you are in Christ, those setbacks can turn into setups right before your eyes. When an opportunity arises, do you think you're capable? When adversity hits, do your thoughts shout "give up?"

To overcome the difficulties, setbacks, fears, rejections, and failures, you must be willing to fight like David. He could no longer stand by and listen to the shouts of Goliath; he had to engage. You too will have to quiet the screams of your giants and face adversity. David's outlook was obviously different compared to the men in Saul's army. Many heard the challenge issued by Goliath, but there was only one whose thoughts enabled him to embrace the moment.

Special God-appointed moments come to all the faithful ones, but our responses must be as deliberate as our actions. During this chapter we will cover three main responses that will prove to be a benefit as you aim to knock out your giants.

1. *Time To Re-Think*

Having the right mindset doesn't come from being beautiful, brilliant, or well built. It's not determined by how much you bench press, or how much money you make. The right mindset comes when you allow the Word of God to transform every wrong thought. The Bible says to take every thought captive to the obedience of Christ, meaning we are to think just like Jesus![1] There was never a situation bigger than Jesus. He knew there was nothing God could not handle. And anytime Satan would try to change His thinking, He would always go back to what God said.

The main reason David was so confident in confronting Goliath was because he had a moment that changed *everything*. I can just imagine the words the prophet Samuel spoke over David; words like, "You're a king", "You're anointed", "You're the one." I'm sure those words echoed over and over in his head. That one moment David had with Samuel was what set him apart for God's service. This is why it is so important for you to get into the Bible; it can provide a moment for you. God has not given us the Bible to read occasionally. It's not just a devotional book; *it's the giant killer*. We must re-think every decision, because our outlook is skewed by our past, our circumstances, and our selfishness. It's time for us to audit our thoughts and start applying the Word so we too can stand against giants.

How else can you explain the courage of David? David wasn't a warrior yet, he was a shepherd. The Word caused him to re-think. He changed from the kid nobody invited to the party to the one who stood before thousands of his countrymen ready to fight a giant everyone feared. For you to embrace the moment, you must re-think. Here are two important thoughts to help you start the process:

• *Don't let what you see produce the wrong thoughts.*
There must be a drastic change in perspective if you're going to fight when others want to flee. The men of Israel saw no chance of winning. These were not incompetent soldiers; they were trained, equipped, and had the necessary skills to fight. By their culture's standards, the army of Israel was the answer for defeating the Philistines. Yet they allowed their thoughts to focus on the size of Goliath rather than God.

This is what happens when people, cultures, and nations try to remove their giants, absent of God's Word. They may show up to the battles, rallies, and summits, but in the end there is nothing they can do. Our nation has had meeting after meeting about violence, teenage pregnancy, drugs, and student illiteracy, yet the giants have not stopped screaming. Just like the army of Israel, it seems we are more concerned about containing the giants rather than destroying them.

Every day you assimilate information. Decisions are made based on what you perceive about the situation you've experienced. With this said, it is easy to only look at the problems instead of finding the solutions. It wasn't that David couldn't see the impressive warrior standing before him. It was this: David knew how to re-think. He knew God was mightier than this giant and his thoughts proved it. **Unless we bring God into our battles, we will never experience true freedom.**

• *You can't pray away your giants.*
One of the biggest concepts we must re-think is the idea that we can pray away our giants. Believers from all over the world are sitting around idly neglecting their moments because

they are too busy praying for God to remove their giants. Now I know that statement may ruffle some religious feathers, so let me clarify. I'm not saying don't pray. In fact, I think we should pray more. We should pray for strength, courage, wisdom, and for God to guide our stones. Remember, just like David, we already have the Word. The Bible says, "if God is for us, who can be against us?"[2]

But there is a crazy thought being circulated among Christians and it's this: "If we just pray, God will do all the work." This is not a completely true statement. Here's an idea: stop praying away your giants; get off your seat and do something about them. I see in the scripture the battle is the Lord's,[3] but we are the saints who enlist. What if the Apostle Paul refused to go on any missionary journeys because he wanted to stay home and pray? What if Martin Luther only prayed and never published the ninety-five theses? Prayer is a vital part in a believer's life, and there are so many powerful principles to learn. Prayer moves the hands of God, but we are His tools. People use prayer as a way of putting all the responsibility on God instead of using it as preparation for the challenge ahead. Remember God wants to use you! **I challenge you to re-think your giants all the way, because the giants in your life are opportunities!**

What Satan means for your harm, God will turn around for your success. Maybe you don't believe me. Well, you're reading a book by someone whose teachers said would never make it. I'm the last person the educated would consider able to write a book. I have no "Dr." by my name. I didn't graduate top of my class. My academic road has been paved with remedial classes, repeating grades, and feeling totally inadequate. In fact, even to this day my spelling needs constant work. Yet by the grace of God I was determined not to let the giant of learning disabilities keep me from sharing what God has done in my life.

What if there was no giant for David to fight? We may have never heard about David. Maybe you're only one giant away from being a household name. Maybe your prayers need to be more of an empowerment rather than a relief.

2. *Don't Be Controlled By The Critics*

It never fails that just about the time you muster up the confidence to embrace the moment, there is someone ready to speak doubt. When David made the announcement to fight Goliath, there was no great applause. In fact, the Bible doesn't mention one person encouraging him to go for it. But it does mention David's own brother Elias and King Saul trying to disqualify him with statements like, "You're too young," and "You're not a warrior." (You can check out this complete dialog beginning at 1 Samuel 17: 28-33.)

You must decide *now* who will control your dreams, victories, and successes, because there are critics surrounding anyone who attempts to battle a giant. There's a big difference between critics and coaches. The critics are people who are ready and willing to find faults, share their opinion, and give harsh and unfair judgments. Critics are more concerned with removing people than promoting people. They're not looking for the giant killer; they're concerned with what happens if the giant wins. If you're not careful, critics can remove your hope and shatter your faith. Coaches are different.

A coach may yell and speak the truth to get the players attention; they may be hard to please, but the function of a coach is to produce *winners.* Coaches are on the sideline encouraging, demanding, and bringing focus to each player. A coach helps improve a player's weak areas. Take a look at the influences in your life: are they coaches or critics? Do they want you to have success? Are they giving you wise counsel or are they just negative?

Taking the necessary steps to *be the one* won't happen without critics. Here are a few concepts I've learned as I've embraced some of my moments:

• *Your value should never be validated by the opinions of others.* If you're going to *be the one*, you can't be swayed by people, praise, or personal attacks. At times it's a struggle to place personal value under the right influence.

Please understand we've been created in the likeness of God. This means we have purpose and value! I don't care who you are, what you've done, where you've grown up, or who has lied to you. Life has value. **You work for influence, but you're born with value.** God is the one who gives value to every life. This is why abortion is such a sin. It tries to reduce the value of life, for what? Personal convenience?

God loves you so much and has great plans for you. The Bible says that His thoughts are good toward you.[4] So the next time you feel the urge to be validated by others, know that you're opening the door for rejection. Why? Because people choose based on what they see, and they may not see someone who is capable.

I mean, let's compare David's physical strength, size, and his ability to that of Goliath. It's a no-brainer; we know who is going to get knocked out, right? Let's face it, by the world's standards, David doesn't look capable. But God saw it differently. David didn't enter into a deep depression because no one believed he could win. This was nothing for David. He had been through this before. He was used to this routine. David knew what he had to do. Critics voicing opinions and comments were not going to stop him. **If you are waiting on everyone else to say "you can," you will be waiting forever.**

• *Not everyone with you will be for you.*

When I was a teenager the phrase, "Can't we all just get along?" was very popular. Sadly the answer is no! Because there are people who want to lead the crowd, and the crowd doesn't want to be lead by just anyone. The crowd wants to be lead by someone who will take them where they are already going; usually somewhere that doesn't require any discomfort. Leadership that wants to turn the crowd around will meet hostility, criticism, and skepticism. **People will disagree with you; this is just part of being the one**. In fact, anytime you make a stand for holiness, the crowd screams grace. When you start talking about faith, the crowd yells work. When you say Ten Commandments, they call you a fundamentalist. *Being the one is about being a leader.* And to be a leader, you must have a short memory when it comes to critics.

Just because people love you doesn't mean they will support your ideas. Don't take it personal when you tell people your dreams and they say it can't be done. Don't let them talk you out of meeting with the giant.

If David would have listened to his brother or even his king, he would have forfeited the opportunity to *be the one*. For David, the fight with Goliath started long before he met him on the battlefield. It started when he made the decision to act. Remember when David's dad didn't see anything special in David? How painful that rejection must have been. When people who are in your corner label you instead of encourage you, it's hurtful. Even Samuel, the man of God, wouldn't have picked David unless God intervened by teaching him how to choose.

• *Don't fight to remove the critics; save your fight for the Goliaths.* When going against a giant, you must be focused on what you're about to do. Don't allow the statements of critics to ring in your head. Give all of those thoughts to the Lord. The Bible says that our fight is not with people; it is with principalities, powers and darkness in high places.[5] We must keep focused on who the real target is. The target is not people who disagree with us or will not support us; the target is the enemy who wants to keep God's people in bondage.

I see so many young people with a chip on their shoulder just waiting to fight anyone who opposes them. This is not the heart of the one! Our fight is not with critics; it's with Goliaths. If you try to change every critic's mindset, then you'll never embrace the right moments. David didn't take out a sword on his brother and demand Eliab to take back his statement. He didn't go to the King and say, "Fine... I quit. All I wanted to do was help, but if you don't think I can, then do it yourself!" David was focused on the giant, not anyone else.

Listen: it's time to stop fighting the wrong battles. It's not your parents, employers, or friends that you should be fighting; it's the giants.

3. React In Faith

As Goliath moved closer to attack David, this young man ran toward the giant. There was no retreat in David. He wasn't second guessing himself. The decision was made and the fight was on. What a moment! Can you imagine the scene as the two were about to engage in combat? It's like an announcer saying, "Let's get ready to ruuuummmmmble!" But before we get too deep into this part of the story, lets back up and look at a few of David's responses.

Faith is always defined when adversity hits. It's easy to speak of faith when everything is going well, but it's during the times of great trouble that your faith is solidified. **For personal faith to hold up in time of great difficulty, it needs to be practiced, built, and applied daily.** It is no surprise that when calamity hits, people run to the Lord. But if you're not careful, the adversity will push you into need, not faith. Need means something is lacking and your focus is on the lack. Faith is knowing that God will provide what you need as long as your trust is in Him.

Let's look at the woman with the issue of blood in the gospel of Matthew. She had a need and her reaction to that need was faith. She knew if she could only touch His cloak she would be healed. The need brought her to Jesus, but that is not why she was healed. If God moved on every need, there would be no needs. God moves on faith. Faith doesn't allow our sight to control the situation. It's a belief in the power of God and an assurance that He wants to answer our request.

David had this type of relationship with the Lord. When no one was around but sheep, David had opportunities to use his faith. This was David's first time on a national stage, but he was no stranger to moments requiring faith. Let's quickly look at two key factors to reacting in faith.

• *Remember your victories.*

When David spoke of fighting Goliath, he wasn't just some passionate kid trying to impress the men of Israel. David knew exactly what he was committing to do because he had a list of moments that God had come through on. And when King Saul questioned his ability to compete against Goliath, David was quick to educate his king on the victories of his past. He told the king about killing the lion and the bear when they came to attack the sheep. Wouldn't you know, the king started changing his tune after he heard about David's successes.

There will be many moments in your life when "it" doesn't look good. But in those times you must remember the faithfulness of God. Just think how many times God has made a way when you thought there was no way. Don't make God start at ground zero with you. If you have a relationship with Him and adversity comes, start at the level you've made it to. Don't go back and start at the beginning as if you're not sure God will or can help.

David allowed each engagement to strengthen his ability to trust the Lord. Now maybe you're a new believer and you haven't experienced all that David had. All I can tell you is open your eyes! The Bible says "that no one comes to the Father except that the Spirit draws him."[6] You've already seen faith in action. When you asked for forgiveness of your sins and asked Jesus to be the Lord of your life, you did this by faith! That means God started a movement and you responded to it! **Don't let the Devil manipulate you into explaining away all your victories.** God is working and has been working. So unleash your faith and watch the giants fall!

• *Let it fly.*

Everyone has goals, visions, and dreams, but what separates the contemplators from the initiators is the ability to embrace the moment. As Goliath was charging toward him, David took out his sling and loaded it with a stone and let it go. David knew the battle was the Lord's. Goliath was insulting the Lord and David knew that God would turn this situation around for His glory. This was not to bring David praise; he was just a chess piece in God's overall plan. However, the point I'm trying to make is that David had the faith to believe he was *the one*.

Stop waiting on the cloud to open up and a sign from heaven to appear before you. Throw your stones. David wasn't concerned with how he looked. He wasn't waiting for a prophetic word. There wasn't any vote that needed to happen. He had the faith to let the rock fly.

Many of you are sitting on ideas, songs, and plans because you're afraid of failing. There are people you know on their way to Hell because you're too intimidated to tell them about Christ. It's not enough to know the right answers. Let's put our money where our mouth is. Throw the stone! Let it fly. God will pick the trajectory and impact of where the stone lands. There is too much potential in the church for our rocks to never take flight.

now is the moment

In every stage of life there are decisions to make on how one will interpret the moments they have been given. The Bible is very clear that "the rain will fall on the just and the unjust".[7] This means every life will experience highs and lows, success and failure, fears and joy, and the chance to overcome them.

Great moments don't happen without adversity. Just like great competition is defined not by the game, but by the teams that play. Maybe you're not facing a physical giant, maybe your giant is a learning disability, forgiving someone who hurt you, breaking an addiction, confronting a harmful relationship, or having a correct view for yourself.

In 1 Samuel 17:26 David dares to ask the question, "What's going to be done for the man who kills this giant?" There are rewards for the ones who embrace the moments. Who will *be the one* to say, "It's my turn?" I can't promise you money, fame, and fortune, but I can tell you that Hebrews 11:6 says that "God is a rewarder of those who diligently seek him."

There will come a time when we all will stand before God and give an account of who we served. And there will be rewards and judgments that will be given out. When this time comes, there will be no opportunity for excuses, noble intensions, and manipulation. The time you have to make a difference is NOW! This is your moment. Stay focused and don't retreat because you are needed! Start today and let's get serious about seeing the giants removed!

The One Who Values Authority

"Have confidence in your leaders and submit to their authority, because they keep watch over you as those who must give an account."

Hebrews 13:17, NKJ

It was a hot, sunny day in Texas. My mom, sister, and I were going to get something to eat. My mom had asked me to take off my hat when we went inside, but I refused. I was fifteen and cared way too much about what others thought. My hat had been on all day and I had hat hair. I mean, come on, how old-school can you get? Take off my hat and risk looking stupid?!

My mom said, "Steven, take off that hat or go sit in the car." So I looked right at her and said to myself, "I'll show her. I just won't eat!" So I went and sat in the car in a hundred degree weather. I was going to show her, and show her I did. I showed her that I didn't value her authority, and it cost me my lunch.Rebellion to authority always costs something. For me it was just lunch. What is rebellion costing you?

Over the years I've come to understand the importance of coming under authority. And one of the concepts I've learned is **lasting influence never comes to the rebellious.** If we fail to value authority, our quest to *be the one* comes to a tragic end. This chapter may not be comfortable to read but it's necessary!

the position of authority

If there is any one topic this culture would push the "dislike" button on, it's authority. We have the "don't tell me what to do" phrase engraved in our minds. From the beginning of mankind, authority has been under attack. No sooner did God finish creation than the devil was persuading man to rebel. Even Jesus was tempted to rebel against the commandments of the Lord. Yet Jesus responded with the Word and sent the devil packing.[1]

I've been asked question after question concerning the topic of authority. As we dive into this chapter, it is vital for us to look at the blessing of authority and deal with the struggles that come from being under authority. Our generation places little value on the position of authority.

A good question to ask is: What are God's thoughts concerning authority? There is no getting around the fact that God promotes and honors those who honor authority. This is why this chapter is so important in our endeavor to *be the one.* We are the ones to value authority. It's difficult learning to be content with checks and balances, but accountability is necessary to have great influence. And without authority, accountability lies dormant.

David's understanding of authority was on a *whole notha level.* He depended on God, not only to fight his battles, but also in his dealing with authority. Before we start with David, let's bring a new character into the mix: Moses. You can read about his leadership starting in Exodus.[2] He is a great example for us as we see how God brings authority in our life to achieve a purpose.

When God wanted to move the children of Israel out of bondage, what did He use? A man! But not just any man. Moses would come under God's authority and show incredible obedience even when he did not understand all that was going on. God could have freed Israel in any way He wanted. Yet He chose a man with a sketchy past to usher them into the land God had waiting. The children of Israel were skeptical when it came to Moses. At first they weren't sure he was the one. Their response was similar to our culture. They grew more and more defiant to the authority God had selected.

We can't continue trashing authority because God has placed them in our lives. Those in authority help lead us to where we could never get by ourselves. Moses was the one God chose to deliver His people and to reestablish a relationship with them. Right now your parents, employers, teachers, and pastors don't do everything right. But like Moses, they are the people God has picked to usher you into more than you could ever imagine.

authority is a gift

God never intended mankind to live without authority. He was the one who instituted authority. In fact, Romans 13: 1-4 says,

> *"[1]Everyone must submit himself to the governing authorities, for there is no authority except that which God has established. The authorities that exist have been established by God. [2]Consequently, he who rebels against the authority is rebelling against what God has instituted, and those who do so will bring judgment on themselves. [3]For rulers hold no terror for those who do right, but for those who do wrong. Do you want to be free from fear of the one in authority? Then do what is right and he will commend you. [4]For he is God's servant to do you good. But if you do wrong, be afraid, for he does not bear the sword for nothing. He is God's servant, an agent of wrath to bring punishment on the wrongdoer."*[3]

God provided authority to govern man. Why? God knew that without authority people would be reckless, totally selfish, and unable to learn obedience. Authority keeps order and has many benefits for us to focus on. Let's look at four benefits that authority brings:

1. Instruction

If you see authority as a benefit, then you will be able to learn from their experiences. I once heard the statement, "You will never repeat what you do not honor." Meaning, every leader has to pay a price for influence. If you're critical and judgmental then it's impossible to walk into the level of influence they have achieved. Good, bad or indifferent, you may not always agree with the authority, but if you don't respect the price they paid to get where they are, you will never experience that level of authority yourself.

Anyone can learn if they're teachable. Don't forget God used Saul to summon David to play for him long before he was known as a warrior. Because of Saul's authority, David was getting the best education possible. This farm boy was learning how to act like a king by being able to watch one. He witnessed Saul at his best and at his worst.

Many in our culture are too busy critiquing and criticizing the authority to learn anything from them. Even if you're learning what not to do, you are still getting an education. So be grateful God has placed you under authority. Learn all you can so you may avoid mistakes and bring proven success into your life.

2. Promotion

The authority in your life has the power to promote you. **Authority can be one of the biggest avenues of blessing in your life.** However, there is a price. I'm not talking about manipulating or "sucking up" to those you're under. Authority will promote you when they can *trust you*. Too many young people feel as if it's their parents' duty to promote them. Parents may love you, but they don't have to promote you. If you want to be promoted, then learn to do the small things well. The Bible says that if you're faithful in the little, you'll be ruler over much.[4]

The devil attacks people in their relationship with authority. He knows that when you come under authority, promotion will come. This ultimately leads to influence. Leaders have the authority and power to promote. A parent can give you an inheritance, pay for college, or put you in the right environment to succeed. Your employer can make you a manager or tell another business owner about you. A teacher can recommend certain opportunities that you could have never achieved yourself. Don't try and do it alone. When you submit to authority, you're not fading into the background. In fact, it may be the very thing that moves you forward.

3.Motivation

Everyone needs to be challenged, pushed, and encouraged to reach for more. The leaders in your life have the ability to press the accelerator and bring the intensity. That pushing spurs growth, change and development. Without authority motivating us to do more, we would become comfortable and complacent. We would never really experience our full potential. Authority can move people when they don't want to move. In the moment, it may seem unfair, unreasonable, or personal but it's exactly what was needed.

Take studying for example. Many times parents are the driving force behind getting all the homework done. Would you have worked as hard without them pushing you to do better? You may not always like when authority pushes you, but if you respond correctly it will pay off.

4.Protection

Without submission to authority, chaos is sure to follow. Man has always needed a physical authority to help him stay on the straight and narrow. Here is a quick rundown of the networks of people God has put in our lives:

- Family[5]
- Parents[6]
- Employers[7]
- Church elders[8]
- Government[9]

Authority can protect you from sin, selfishness, and pride. Authority wants to protect you by seeing from a different perspective. I know it is frustrating when the authority tells you "No" or doesn't go with your idea. But just ask yourself the question, "Has authority ever protected you?" What about that guy or girl you wanted to date and your parents said no? It was heartbreaking, but later you found out what kind of player they really were. Do you really want every authority in your life to say "Yes" to your ideas or to agree with your perspective? No way! If that happened it would be self-destructive. **Authority is not sent to agree with you but to protect you.**

Everyone is going to come under some authority. God didn't establish authority to be a terrible part of your life. God loves you! Don't resist the authority God has put you under, embrace it.

time to yield

Submitting to authority is never easy. But if you're going to *be the one,* submitting is a sure way to influence. With the leaders God has put you under, are you yielding your will to promote them or is it all about you? It's when you learn to yield your selfish desires that God takes notice. It speaks of the motivation of your heart. Just like driving a car, yielding is when you give way to the other vehicle who has the right to be first. Authority has been given the right to speak and be heard, even if you don't agree.

You can never be God's leader unless you learn how to yield to His authority, His Spirit, and His commandments. If you won't obey, you're not yielding! The *one* gains and maintains influence by their willingness to yield to authority.

don't get it twisted

It was about 1:30 in the morning and I was working at Cinemark Movie Theater in Waco, Texas. The manager and I had just got done previewing the movie "Twister." It was projected to be a blockbuster. In fact, we had already started selling advance tickets and had the 7 o'clock showing sold-out for Friday night. About halfway through the movie, there was a mis-frame. (That is when the movie was spliced wrong and caused the viewer to see two frames.) So being the incredible servant that I was, I told the manager I would go and fix it. It was late and he said to me, "Steven, don't worry about the film. I will fix it in the morning." But I knew what he meant. What he really meant was, "I wish someone would fix the mis-frame!" After all, going home when there was work to do was not my mindset. I was there to help and help I would. I went right up to the projector that had the movie on it and started fixing "Twister." It wasn't long before my boss paged me on the phone and said, "What are you doing?" So I said, "Just cleaning up a bit." (Little did he know. Haha)

I fixed the mis-frame and started the movie again. So it could be able to start from the beginning for tomorrow's showings. As the movie was running through, I went down to his office and we started talking. He finally said, "Man, I'm ready to go. Let's get out of here." I said, "No problem, let me just go shut down the projector because I fixed the mis-frame." He looked at me and said, "What? I told you I would do it in the morning. Go turn it off."

As I was walking up the stairs, the projector was smoking and the movie was on the ground. We're talking yards and yards of film that was totally... twisted. I ran to the phone and buzzed him to come up quickly. It was a bad deal. He looked at the movie on the ground and said, "WHAT DID YOU DO?" He was so mad. Over and over again he kept saying, "I told you not to."

I had such good intentions! I just wanted to help him. Yet, I didn't listen to authority and it cost me my job. It was such a bad deal that the company started an investigation to see if I was hired by their competition. I guess people get mad when you mess up a 25,000 dollar movie. By the way, the investigation proved that it was faulty equipment.

Too many times we have a different idea than authority does. It's not that my idea was bad, it was just bad timing. The movie may have broken either way but by not submitting to the manager, it made everything my fault. There will be times that you will blow it with authority, but you must allow those times to teach you. Don't get into the… "but"... stuff. You know the "but" word comes out when authority makes a statement that has some error in it. Don't have an overactive justifier, just take your part of the responsibility and move on.

I could have blamed it on the projector, but the bottom line was, I was doing something I was told not to do. There was no malice in my heart. I was trying to help, but it was still disobedience. It's important for us to follow the instructions that authority gives us because it proves that we are faithful and can be trusted. If you always have a better idea, most likely you have some leadership potential. However, if you always act on your better idea, usurping your authority, you're not the leader that God is looking for. God picks people who know how to follow. If you can't yield to the physical authority, how will you be able to yield to the spiritual authority? Train yourself to do exactly what is said and then watch the favor come.

two wrongs don't make a right

Probably the hardest time to honor authority is when they are wrong because let's face it, all human authority is, in fact, human. Authority is prone to making mistakes and we are the ones who have to work through the wrongs in order to keep a right perspective. To honor authority doesn't mean you have to agree with them, but you do have to respect the position they hold. David understood how hard it is to keep the respect for authority when the choices they make are wrong.

Everything was going great for David. The dude had just killed Goliath, he was placed as the military commander right under Saul, and people were starting to sing songs about how great he was. You know you're doing something right when people you don't know start to sing songs about you. David was at the top of his game. Life couldn't be any better, but over time Saul started to get jealous. His anger started to flare up and he began to resent David.

There was one time when David was playing the harp to help soothe the king's spirit, when Saul lost it. He flipped out on David and threw a spear at him. That's right, a SPEAR! Can you imagine standing up playing your heart out for the king? Then all of a sudden he gets ticked off and throws a spear at you? I guess Saul didn't like the song! I don't know about you, but there are a lot of wrongs I can forgive. BUT A SPEAR! REALLY?! David wasn't a nobody anymore. He was the one who removed the giant and this is how Saul treats him? No way! Where is the respect?! Did David have to take this? No, but he did. And this was just the beginning of Saul and David's fallout.

Saul tried to kill David many times. Yet David never spoke against the king, never attacked him, and even when everyone else wanted David to destroy him, David wouldn't! David's response to authority was mind-blowing. What Saul did was as wrong as it could be, but David never fought the authority God had put him under. He only fled when there was no hope that he couldn't escape imminent physical death. David could have rebelled against Saul and have been justified in man's eyes. But he yielded to the position God had put Saul in. Just because David had a few victories, he still hadn't taken his position as king. God was using Saul to train David, regardless of how David felt about it. Something was happening in David, even through the wrong actions of Saul.

Don't be so quick to stand in judgment with your authority, because it will lure you into rebellion. When authority is wrong, it's not your job to teach them or critique them. God will fight your battles, but it won't be in your timing. It seems like we always want God to act quickly when other people are mistreating us, but want grace when we are the ones at fault. God gives all authority time to change, re-evaluate, and repent. If they won't listen God will remove them. You don't have to worry about God's part, just yours. The Bible says, "God will not be mocked".[10]

Taking on authority is not your battle, it is the Lord's. So the next time your parents say the wrong thing, take it and dish it back to the Lord. Next time your boss falsely accuses you, take it and dish it. Because when you fire back with attacks of your own, you're just as wrong.

Now I'm not talking about taking abuse or physical harm. David ran for his life because it was the only way to survive, but he never attacked the king. This generation must stop attacking their authority and start honoring it. Start today. Throw down all the accusation you've compiled against authority releasing it into the hands of God. This is the right response for the one!

fighting through the offense

It is so easy to take on the wrong attitude when dealing with authority, especially when their instructions or responses are not what you expected. For you to demand your parents, pastors, teachers, or employers to make every right call is not going to happen. To assume that they will always agree with your reasoning is naive.

It's amazing how many hurt believers we have in the body of Christ. Yes, I know there have been some bad spiritual leaders, but come on. We must learn to fight through offense just like a boxer has to fight through being hit in order to get the KO. Offenses are being thrown at you all the time. Will you learn how to take them? Will you fire back out of emotion or cast those hurts, rejections and misunderstandings on the Lord. **Don't allow offenses to stop you from getting your KO's for the Kingdom.** Train yourself how to react and respond correctly.

With all the struggle between Saul and David, it's amazing that David could keep the right heart. But David a had great understanding of the value of authority. He refused to allow his flesh to come against what God had chosen:

> *"So David and Abishai went to the army by night, and there was Saul, lying asleep inside the camp with his spear stuck in the ground near his head. Abner and the soldiers were lying around him. Abishai said to David, 'Today God has delivered your enemy into your hands. Now let me pin him to the ground with one thrust of my spear; I won't strike him twice.' But David said to Abishai, 'Don't destroy him! Who can lay a hand on the LORD's anointed and be guiltless? As surely as the LORD lives,' he said, 'the LORD himself will strike him; either his time will come and he will die, or he will go into battle and perish. But the LORD forbid that I should lay a hand on the LORD's anointed. Now get the spear and water jug that are near his head, and let's go.'"*[11]

David could have been offended. After all, Saul was trying to kill him. If it had been me, it would be really hard not to think, "Look at the spear! Yeah…It's my turn now! It's time to show you what's up!" But those thoughts would have been unproductive.

Anytime you dwell on offense, it works its way into your heart. David never allowed his action to make a move of aggression against Saul. Why? Because David valued Saul's position and knew it was anointed! There may be a few times in your life that the position of the authority needs to be more respected than the person. You will disagree with your authority, but what does their position mean? Don't allow their shortcomings or wrong choices to place you in bondage.

Remember, don't take everything personally. Your emotional freedom is too expensive. It's time for this generation to get tough! Stop whining about how mistreated you are and let's change the world! Take the focus off of you and put it on making a difference.

when can I lead my own life?

Many think that being under authority is forfeiting the management of their life. They only see authority as people trying to control them by telling them what to do. Not true! That is a rebellious mindset. Authority is not in your life to steal your individuality. Authority is not trying to control you. Did your mom follow you to school today and question every one of your decisions? Did your Pastor show up with his stopwatch clocking how much time you spent with the Lord today? Does your employer demand that you act, dress, and communicate just like him? No! In fact, daily you make countless decisions that your authority doesn't seek to control.

The problem is we want total control. Because then we can do anything we want, whenever we want. In the next chapter, we will see that David found himself in the place of total control and it cost him. Authority is not the enemy. It is there to help you on your road to becoming a productive adult. Do you want to learn everything the hard way? There are many bumps and bruises that you can avoid by listening to the right leaders.

Take a minute and evaluate the responses you've made to the leaders around you. What would they say about your ability to yield? Are you such a leader that you can't be led? Are you so opinionated about the leadership in your church that it's causing you to be stagnant?

Authority is not holding you back. They are trying to set you up. Resist the temptation to rebel. Resist the temptation to fire back. Yes, there will be times when you'll be angry, misunderstood, and rejected, but the benefits of authority far outweigh the negatives. The devil will always push you into doing it "my way". Don't fall into that trap of pride. **Allow yourself to be led and the season will come when you will *be the one* leading others.**

The One Wrong Place

"A wise man fears and departs from evil, but a fool rages and is self confident ."

Proverbs 14:16 (NKJV)

It was a time when kings went to war and David sat in his palace while his men went to battle. As he was strolling through the palace, he made his way to the top of the roof. There he saw her. She was bathing, beautiful, and rockin' the birthday-suit. This woman was HOT! She was all day fine! She was a neck-popping, double-take woman. That's when you turn your head so fast to look that you strain your neck and even though it hurts, you have to look twice. This girl had it going on!

As if this peep show wasn't enough, David went a step further. He called his servant to bring the woman to him. That one moment led to an affair with another man's wife and her becoming pregnant. His night of passion brought years and years of consequences, trouble, and hardship.[1]

I'm sure David went back and forth trying to convince himself not to look at Bathsheba, but his desires were speaking to him louder than his calling. Those desires were pushing him into a very wrong place which started a shameful series of actions. David felt like the only way to crawl out of the wrong place was by covering up his sin. This ultimately lead to the killing of Uriah, the husband of Bathsheba. But the consequences didn't stop there. Soon after Uriah was killed, the baby died, David's family unraveled, and his oldest son tried to kill him.[2]

David found himself in a place he should have never been. He was supposed to be at war. That's where all the kings were, but not David. Perhaps David was tired. Maybe he thought this excursion wasn't worthy of his attendance. Could it be that he thought he had already experienced enough great moments? Either way, David was staying at home while his men fought his enemies. Plain and simple, David was in the wrong place. He was anointed to lead and fight, yet he was home relaxing in the palace. No leading, no fighting, just resting.

think about the cost

Great moments come and go, but your legacy will be defined by the decisions you make daily. Don't ever think,

"It's just one time" or "I won't get caught." The Bible says that "Everything that is hidden shall be revealed."[3] Meaning you can't continue to visit wrong places and think it won't cost you. When you take the challenge to *be the one*, you have to know that the Devil doesn't like it. He is hoping that you will get tired of the daily fight and decide to rest. The enemy waits for you to let down your guard so he can strike a powerful blow that will shatter your influence.

What was David thinking? Had he forgotten he was the one? What can we possibly learn from him now? I believe we may uncover one of the greatest lessons ever learned. It doesn't matter how many victories you've had or the amount of faith you've operated in. No matter how many right decisions you've made, anyone can find himself in the wrong place. We must be constantly aware of the direction we are travelling and what destination we're headed for. David was now a king, but even a king's rule cannot stop the consequences of wrong choices.

where are you looking?

Most wrecks happen because of broken focus and a lack of attention. The Bible says "keep our eyes on Jesus, the author and finisher of our faith."[4] Like when you're driving, it is imperative that you keep your eyes on the road. Looking in the wrong places can lead to wrong turns, missing crucial warning signs, or major damage. It's not enough for us to know how to navigate a vehicle. We must give continual focus if we're to avoid the dangers that lie ahead.

If you've been in church any number of years, you have learned the importance of prayer, Bible reading, and worship. Although these help you navigate, you still have to steer the vehicle in the direction you know you need to go.

For example, a few years ago my son and daughter received a toy four-wheeler for Christmas. This brought about two huge challenges: keeping their focus forward and saving the one year old from getting run over. Because my kids were young, they got side-tracked easily. They loved to turn their heads and talk to me while they were driving, so I was constantly telling them, "Don't look at me; watch where you are going." They've hit trees, our dog, and yes, even the one year old, all because they weren't looking where they were going.

It is so easy to get distracted with what is going on around us. **If we don't guard where we're looking, just like David, we will find ourselves in potentially harmful places.** The desire of David's heart was to be a godly king. He wasn't trying to hurt God. It was just a weak moment. But understand this: weak moments can leave huge scars. David allowed his attention to be captivated on something that was not his to have. If we're not careful we will start out driving in one direction and half way through the trip begin looking in another. This, my friend, is a recipe for disaster. Countless young Christians are leaving through the back door of the church because their eyes have been fixed on something that seems more attractive than living a godly life.

They have been bombarded with opinions from sources like social networking, media, and music which convince them to believe thoughts like: "Live however you want," "Never deny your desires," "You only live once," and "Do it or you'll regret it."

In the end, it's always the young people who are affected by this kind of philosophy. I meet countless teenagers struggling with self image, searching for acceptance, and feeling rejected. Why? Because some friend, parent, or family member lost focus on what was truly important. Our focus must stay on a desire to see the Lord. This is the only way we can *be the one* to hear "well done good and faithful servant".[5] We can't afford to have our attention captured and our message lost. There are three ways to ensure your eyes are fixed ahead:

1. Evaluate What Has Your Attention

Being the one is not just pushing down the accelerator hoping to quickly achieve your purpose. The process of transformation takes time. It's about taking the necessary actions to ensure that you end up in the right place. So yes, the accelerator is a big part, but so is the steering wheel, engine, and brakes.

In every car, the brakes play a vital part in reaching our destination. From time to time, things get in the way, distractions happen, and we need to make a sudden stop. However, stops only happen if we are paying attention. For example:

• If someone has done you wrong, it can become your center of attention. If it does, then offense is sure to follow. Offense will always affect your thoughts and actions. It produces a roadblock between you and being the one.

• I know popularity is sooooooo important (very sarcastic) ...but what is it demanding from you? The pursuit of popularity is probably leaving you with little time and energy. If your Bible is dusty and you can't remember the last time you really connected with God, then you may need to adjust your schedule.

• If a dating relationship is distracting you from being the one then break up! God loves relationships and He created us to need them, but know this: if any relationship comes before Him, it is sure to lead you to the wrong place.

• Our nation is drowning in debt. The "buy it now, pay later" mindset keeps us working to pay off the debt and demands us to shop for the next thing we "have to have." These thoughts take us to a wrong place. It keeps us unable to pay attention to the leadings of the Holy Spirit, which are meant to keep us on track.

Allow this to be your wake up call. A wreck may be coming. Avoid it! Make no mistake about it, David wanted to look in the wrong direction! It's so easy to convince yourself that the wrong places are OK or not that bad. That's why you must constantly evaluate and ask yourself the hard questions, "Is the attention I'm giving to this area in my life propelling me forward or pushing me backward?" If you don't like the answer you come up with, hit the brakes. Listen, a quick stop is better than a wreck going 75 mph.

2. Keep A Focal Point

The key to any successful journey is to know where you're going and then chart the best course. It's simple really: once you know your destination, your focus becomes fixed on the roads, routes, and exits needed to complete the journey. For a moment, David forgot his destination. His point of focus became Bathsheba, not the Lord.

Temptations and adversity often cause us to change our focus, but you must be strong. Allow the Holy Spirit to help you in your time of trouble. Don't forget, God is strong when we are weak.[6] No matter what comes up, don't dethrone Jesus as Lord by placing something else before Him. Keep Him as your focal point.

It's great to have goals. Whatever you choose to become don't allow it to take over your life. Very quickly your goals can become your total focus. Remember, don't let the things of this world creep up and take first place. Keep that position reserved for Christ and His message. Nothing the world has to offer will satisfy you. Not money, fame, a great job or even an awesome family can fulfill you. If you make the things of this world your total focus you're inviting hurt into your life. Why? Because everything the world provides will change. But God says that "I change not".[7] "He is the same yesterday, today and forever".[8] He is consistent! If your focal point is Him and His message then blessing and understanding are sure to follow. Take a look at these verses in Mark 6:32-34. Pay close attention to the part in bold print:

> *"So they went away by themselves in a boat to a solitary place.* ***But many who saw them leaving recognized them and ran on foot from all the towns and got there ahead of them.*** *When Jesus landed and saw a large crowd, he had compassion on them, because they were like sheep without a shepherd. So he began teaching them many things."*[9] *(emphasis added)*

Look at what the crowd's reaction was when Jesus and the disciples were leaving. They NOTICED! It's almost like a few people saw that Jesus and the boys were leaving and said, "Hey something is going on; Jesus is getting in a boat...Let's follow Him." How cool would it have been to announce to everyone that Jesus was departing? Someone in that crowd was focused on Jesus. What He was doing and where He was going became somebody's focal point. When Jesus becomes your focal point, your commitment will be seen by how you follow. **Those who lay aside distractions and focus on following Christ will have the opportunity to walk in real influence.**

3. Stay Away From "Me" Moments

For us to stay heading straight, we must control our desires. Uncontrolled desires will always move us into sin. Sin is knowingly breaking God's standards and putting ourselves above Him. Let's just call the action of sin as taking a "me" moment. It's grounded in selfish and fleshly desires.

Like children who know they're not supposed to get a cookie from the cookie jar, they plot and plan for the perfect timing. And as soon as the parents are out of the way, they strike. Like a stealth ninja, they make their way to the cookie jar, consuming cookie after cookie, hoping no one will ever know. Many may argue that it is just a cookie, but the issue is not the cookie. The issue is it's a "me" moment. It's rooted in deception and if left unattended will move away from just cookies to something much worse.

"Me" moments always take you to the wrong places. And worse, they affect the ones you love. It's not just your life. We all have a responsibility to those who are in our lives. Our friends, siblings, parents, and mates will all be affected by selfish acts. Remember, to *be the one* you must care!

David's "me" moment took him to the wrong place. Now, can God forgive? Yes! Will God restore? Yes! But consequences don't go away just because you repent. The sting of "me" moments can continue to be felt long after repentance has happened.

Please understand one sin will not destroy you, but it can start an enslavement process. All sin leads to captivity and a lifestyle of sin that will remove you from the presence of God. This is why compromising is so dangerous. It sets up a roadblock detouring you from the place God wants you to be. Compromise is always an enemy to a life of influence. It gives allowances for wiggle-room based on the thought "no one will ever know."

David found himself in the wrong place because he was looking at his desires. In hind sight it's easy for us to see he could have avoided the distraction and all the consequences that came with it. We must take his example and stay alert. Watch the road because wrong turns lead to wrong places.

master the art of a U-turn

The best way to leave a wrong place is to never be there. However, you and I both know that everyone visits wrong places. Romans 3:23 says, "for all have sinned…"[10] No matter how many times you've visited the wrong place or how far you've veered off track, you don't have to stay lost. You can turn around.

One of the most effective ways to turn around is by applying the perfected skill of a U-turn. Over the last few years my travelling has picked up and there have been moments when a U-turn was necessary. No matter where I am, a U-turn enables me to turn around. Before a U-turn is attempted one must first discover they're going the wrong way.

David refused to admit the wrong he had done until a prophet came and rebuked him. This prophet told David that God knew everything he had done and that there would be consequences for his actions. There was no hiding now.

Everything was out in the open. What would David's response be to the truth he was given? Would he justify his position? Would he demand the prophet to leave? After all, David was king. No! David fell to his knees and said, "I have sinned against God."[11] He didn't talk back, fight, or get offended. David didn't say to the prophet, "Stop judging me." He was broken and started to repent. Repentance is just like that U-turn. When you repent, it is an acknowledgement of where you've been, followed by a change in direction.

What is your response to the truth? Do you come clean and allow the correction to help you? Or when you're caught, do you try and hide the truth hoping to keep parts of the matter concealed? Please understand that correction is not rejection. Correction is not always fun, but it is necessary to be used by God to do great things. God loves you and the Bible says that "those who I love, I correct".[12] Getting caught in a wrong place is not the worst thing! It's not getting caught that should bother you. Getting caught could save your life and give you the opportunity for redemption. When truth comes, own up and don't cover up. It's your personal freedom that is at stake.

The point of a U-turn is to get you back on course. Maybe this last year you've had one "me" moment after another and it could be that no one knows. Take my advice, avoid the wreck. Make whatever course adjustment needed to get back on the right road. Allow the words in this book to resonate in your ears and touch your heart. There is much work to do and people are counting on you to *be the one*.

Instead of quickly racing though this chapter let's apply the brake for a minute. Allow the Holy Spirit to correct, convict, communicate, and comfort you. I don't know where you are, but my hope is that this chapter has awakened your spirit and re-focused your attention. Your life doesn't have to be defined by wrong choices and wrong places. Evaluate the road you are on and what is truly important. The wrong place looks fun, exciting, and appealing but it always costs more than any can afford to pay. Join me right now and let's make a turn that God would honor. Repeat this prayer and say goodbye to those wrong places.

Dear Heavenly Father, thank you for reviving my spirit by showing me the areas of my life that are causing me harm. Lord, my heart desires to avoid the wrong places in life. Right now, I humbly repent from my selfish choices and actions. Restore me and help me as I strive to make all necessary changes so my life brings you glory. Thank you for the gift of your Son and His death that make me clean before you. Now, take my hands and prepare me to **be the one** *to help change this generation. In Jesus' name, Amen.*

The One Real Commitment

"I will not hide your righteousness in my heart; I will speak of your faithfulness and salvation. I will not conceal your love and your truth from the great assembly."

Psalm 40:10

There is no question that the spiritual condition of our nation has been progressively retreating from Biblical truth. The call to *be the one* is more than just a fad or catchy cliché. My prayer is that it would start as a movement and progress into a lifestyle. We can no longer compartmentalize our faith. The two-world system has got to go. We can't live a Christian lifestyle around certain people and then quickly change our standards around others. God is looking for someone to engage in a real commitment. Someone who doesn't base their spiritual walk on how they feel or what pressure they are going through.

Are commitments hard to keep? Do they take work? Do you ever feel like you want to quit? The answer to all three is, "Yes." But a good, legitimate commitment, if kept, will always produce great rewards.

I think that's why I'm so into David and his quest to *be the one*. For David, it was never about being king; it was about serving God no matter what that entailed. His job descriptions for life included:

- Son
- Brother
- Shepherd
- Harp player
- Servant
- Soldier
- Friend
- Husband
- Father
- King

However, the greatest title he was given was the one God gave him, "Man after my own heart." "And when He had removed Saul, He raised up for them David as king, to whom also He gave testimony and said, 'I have found David the son of Jesse, a man after My own heart, who will do all My will.'"[1] David's heart longed to bring God honor.

Life and titles will constantly change as we grow, but your commitment to *be the one* should remain the same. Just like David, the decision is yours. Who will you serve? David kept his commitment to serve and honor God to the end of his life. In his last big moment as king, David is talking to his son Solomon and he gives him this wisdom:

"And keep the charge of the Lord your God, to walk in His ways, to keep His statutes, His commandments, His ordinances and His testimonies, according to what is written in the law of Moses, that you may succeed in all that you do and wherever you turn."[2]

As those last words echoed in Solomon's ears, David's heart is heard loud and clear. He basically said, "Son, if you want to prosper, commit yourself to walk in the ways of the Lord." Let those same words resonate deep within you as you commit to serve God.

more than a ceremony

When Katie and I got married it was truly a sight to behold. The day could not have gone any better. Katie and I were surrounded by our very best friends in the world. The sanctuary was full of family and friends. As the music started, my wife-to-be started walking down the center aisle. My attention was captivated. She was beautiful, radiant, and stunning. As we stepped up to the stage and the minister began to speak, it became very clear to me that this ceremony wasn't just a party or get together. This ceremony was based on the notion that a lifelong commitment was being made. When I said "I do" to my wife, I meant it. It doesn't matter if I get tired, frustrated, angry, or hurt. I made a real commitment.

Our ceremony lasted about forty-five minutes, but the commitment that was made in that moment is to last a lifetime. The words we spoke and the decision we made will long outlast the ceremony. In fact, we are closer, more in love, and more like-minded than when we made the commitment on our wedding day.

The reason for this example is not just to give you the history of Steven and Katie Sexton. I'm using this to show you that making the commitment is just one of many special moments. As believers, our goal is to live beyond the ceremony. For us, accepting salvation is often shared by friends, family, or our churches. There is such a freedom and an emotional exchange that happens when you understand the love and grace of God. Many times I see people make a decision for Christ but after the initial moment has faded, the commitment fades as well. Following Christ and keeping Him Lord of our lives takes work if we are going to keep our commitment. Work is not a bad thing! Work provides blessing and advancement. If I don't work on my marriage… trust me, it's not good. There aren't any golden stars given out for making a commitment. It's keeping the commitment that's impressive.

This is where the person who commits to *be the one* steps in to help discover, develop, and deploy believers to reach their God-given purpose. For Katie and me, it wasn't just a rash statement, deluded in emotion. We had considered the cost of what it would take to have a good marriage. We understood that without work the ceremony would have been our only great moment.

understand the task

Before you embark on accomplishing any task, it's always good to find out how much dedication is needed in order to complete it. For anything to be achieved, it can only happen with a strong commitment. The walls of a home must stay attached to the foundation for the structure to hold up. An employer will only give raises or a promotion to the employee who is dedicated. How attached and dedicated is your commitment to follow Christ? God is moving this generation of believers into a greater level of anointing. But for Him to entrust us with that anointing, our commitment can't be limited to church services and Sunday mornings. Our quest to *be the one* will have to take preeminence over our personal agenda.

When we truly engage in fulfilling our real commitment, change will not only begin in our lives but in the lives of others around us. How exciting is it that God allows us to partner with His plan? It very exciting. In fact, it's life changing. Yet, average Christianity doesn't understand this type of commitment. They sit back and hope someone else will pay the price. I believe you are the one to bring His message to this generation. However, this will only happen when you understand the commitment.

This commitment should change everything about you. How you think, act and respond will become totally different. Because of my commitment to Katie there were some major changes that happened in my life. For example, I could no longer act like a single man going anywhere, anytime I wanted. All of my friends became guys because I wanted to shut any door that could hurt our marriage. My conversation changed because I started using the phase "let me check with my wife."

I say all this to help you understand the task of being the one. Let's really look at your commitment to Christ. Is it full of empty promises and noble intentions? Do you see your commitment changing how you live? What message of His burns inside you now that you have fully committed to Him? People who understand the benift of serving Christ feel compelled to communicate it. This is not just a one time sign up. Just like marriage, your committment should not be made based solely on emotion, but on a right understanding of what it will take to live this new life.

Once this revelation has made its way into your heart it must be acted upon. To *be the one* we must take His message and work it, think about, operate in it and reproduce it. How you live should prove your promises. Don't let your faith just be a spiritual sound bite. Let it be something you do. When what you commit to starts to be re-producted into others that is living your promise. You can only reproduce what has been produced in your own life. Don't allow your commitment to Christ to fall short. Give the attention needed to act on your committment.

stay connected

A commitment made without investing time is a surface commitment at best. In our busy lives it's hard to find an opening in our schedule to connect with God. We have school, friends, work and even church that demand our presence. On top of that we have Facebook, Twitter, blogs we read, and text messages to answer. It's like we are prisoners to our schedules. If that is not enough then add to the mix music, movies, and other types of entertainment. This culture has a way of multitasking like none before it. However, God is not one of many options. He doesn't ride shotgun. He is the driving force. Our priorities, which are many, can't rob him of placement.

None of the things I've mentioned above are bad things. In fact, they are fun and make life more interesting. But even good things can move into a position that they shouldn't take. For you to *be the one* it's necessary to take the time to connect with God. Just like in a boy/girlfriend relationship, if there is no connection you lose interest. We have to MAKE TIME for the Lord.

Meaning, you schedule a meeting with God. Just like with your friends, take God out for coffee. Talk to God for two hours and look down at your watch and be shocked that time went by so fast. When something funny or painful happens, talk to Him. Be careful about the good things that can divide your heart, causing a surface commitment. Wake up to the idea that you can make an appointment with God. Set a time to turn off all the things that demand your attention and stay connected.

quitting is not an option

My goal is not to overwhelm you! It's to show you how important a deep connection with God can be. Going to church can make you feel a sense of deep commitment. But what is that producing? A relationship with God always produces fruit. **What you produce proclaims your priorities.** Don't get discouraged because of shortcomings and failures. God loves doing outrageous works through imperfect people.

We know David made some really big mistakes. But I'll tell you this, David may have failed many times, but he never quit. Perseverance is a must if we're going to complete God's assignments. James 1:12 says, "Blessed is the man who perseveres under trial, because when he has stood the test, he will receive the crown of life that God has promised to those who love Him."[3] The key to perseverance is understanding the end objective. In this case the end objective is complete salvation, personal relationship, transformation, and God's presence. It's this understanding that will keep you when boredom, pressure, hurt, or failure want to cause you to give up. God is looking for believers who *never say*... "I quit."

In 2010 the New Orlean Saints shocked the world by winning the NFL Superbowl XLIV. The remarkable story of perseverance by the city, organization, players, and fans is definitely one to be retold. After twenty years of having a losing record, fans started to wear brown paper bags over their heads because of the embarrassment. The team was so bad many fans of football started calling the Saints the Ain'ts. Being a huge Dallas Cowboys fan (How 'bout them Cowboys?) even I jumped in on the fun. On top of all of that we all remember in 2005, when hurricane Katrina slammed into the city. The force and pressure broke the levies and flooded the city. It was the worst natural disaster in US history. Yet through all the obstacles and setbacks the Saints didn't quit. New Orleans didn't quit!

Why are we tempted to quit? Is it because we get bored? Maybe it's because there are not enough new experiences to keep us interested. It could be that people quit because they get tired or they no longer see a benefit to all their effort.

We all know the routine! We sign up for the glamour and the fun of a great opportunity, and then the mundane sets in. So we back out and lose interest because the excitement is gone. Truthfully, it's always easier to start a new commitment than it is to stay hooked up to the commitment we've already made. Listen, the world tries to convince you that there is something better than making a commitment to God. That's why there's such a strong pull on you to walk away or give up. Don't hurt your relationship with God by losing your passion to follow. Remember His way is truth. Nothing this world has is better than what God can give you. Don't let anything come between you and Him.

If you have thoughts concerning your commitment to God you are not alone. We've all been tempted to walk away. Many have felt the restrictions of the Christian life and wanted to throw in the towel. Because from time to time we get caught up in all "the don'ts." However, just stop and think; when we accept Christ, we get the do's. We do: get to be forgiven, have a personal relationship with God, walk in authority over the enemy, have our requests heard by God, and share a message that brings freedom to others. When you stay committed to the plan of God the only one to lose is the Devil.

Let's fight against the thoughts that say "this is too hard." And know that anything worth doing will take effort and moments of discomfort. In fact, Jesus and Peter had a conversation along these same lines. Jesus was talking about eating His body and drinking his blood in the book of John, and Peter came up to Jesus and said, "Hey bro, can we tone this down a little? People are thinking you're crazy!" But Jesus said, "This is the message and the reason I came, if you don't like it, you can leave." Peter's response was perfect; he said, "What? I have no other place to go."[4] Peter knew even though following Jesus wasn't easy, it was way better than the alternative. Peter kept his commitment that altered the direction of his life and so can you.

I say this to implore you to never give up! Never quit on God. And never quit on what you're believing God for.

Many of you may be praying for a loved one to be saved, healed, or set free, so don't you dare give up and quit! Stay committed! Stay faithful! And let's change the course of this generation.

The One To Make A Difference

"Therefore go and make disciples of all nations, baptizing them in the name of the Father and of the Son and of the Holy Spirit,"

Matthew 28:19

Okay so you're probably feeling like, "Yes, I'm so jazzed about being the one." And you've finally made it to the last chapter. Well, hold on to that excitement because we are about to take this baby to a new level. I'm talking about the apostle level. An apostle means one who is sent. Right before Jesus departed from the world He gave them a mission. He wanted them to take the truth and communicate it. Each of us know young people who need to hear the truth of the Gospel. This is the mandate of the One—to care enough to be inconvenienced. The time has come for Spirit-filled believers to leave their mark.

You have the capacity to leave a legacy. Don't underestimate God. He is willing and ready to work through you. Put away the fear and make the decision to reproduce all that God has put inside you. Remember He is the substance and we are the vessel. Meaning, it's not us that bring forth transformation in people lives; it's Him.

Right now there are countless teens just waiting to hear the truth. This is not your pastor's responsibility, it's yours. No matter what age you are there is someone in your circle of influence that you can impart truth into. They may even be a few years younger than you so don't overlook them. They are the ones you can leave a mark on.

your signature please

Any time I use my visa card my signature is required. My signature is a way of showing the credit company that I am authorizing my purchase. In fact, any time you buy something major there is a contract drawn up and your signature must be given. Your signature shows that you approve. And in the case of our founding fathers, it showed commitment. If it weren't for the signatures of the 56 men in the Continental Congress, the Declaration of Independence would've never happened. Their signatures made the vision of the United States a reality. Your signature shows what you stand for and what you promote.

Your life is a signature and it is to be read in the hearts of people. Your life counts. What mark are you leaving? How can we see your signature on the world?

In 2007 in Pasadena California, McKay Hatch started the "No Cussing Club." He was bothered by the cussing around him and one day challenged his friends to stop. This club was started to help those who didn't know how to stop cussing. One month later he had 50 enrolled in the club. Then it moved to 100 members. He created a website and set a goal to get members in every state. Six months later that goal was reached and it grew to 10,000 members. The media soon picked up the phenomena which sky rocketed the club's membership to well over 20,000 people. By the way, McKay started this when he was 14. Wow! Don't tell Mckay he's too young.[1] Check out this next story about a TWELVE YEAR OLD!

Craig Keilberger, a 12-year-old Canadian boy, started his own organization called Free the Children. It all started when he read a story about a young Indian boy who was killed as a result of being sold into child labor. This is when Craig decided to leave his mark. His cause became clear as he spoke to his classroom and started passing around some petitions to political leaders and heads of corporations. Along with his friends he began raising money by speaking to various community groups. He began to work on setting free an Indian Prime Minister who was imprisoned for his work against child labor. Once he succeeded in that, his organization flourished. Today he travels around the world and Free the Children currently affects twenty-seven countries. He speaks in front of thousands of people in order to raise funds to save the lives of children around the world.[2]

Both of these young men made the choice to permanently write their signature in the hearts of the people they helped. Now it's your turn to *be the one* and leave your mark. Below are three ways to make a lasting impact on the lives around you.

1. Discover

I remember when I discovered girls. All of a sudden it was like, "Wow" something had changed. I was getting all nervous. There were love songs playing in my head. I didn't know how to talk. My heart was beating so fast! And this was in the third grade! (Cuz that's how I do!)

I also remember when I discovered how much stuff costs. When I was young I had no concept of money. I didn't understand the difference between a dollar and a hundred dollars. If I saw something I wanted, I asked, whined, and begged for it. But once I started to work, the concept of spending money was totally different.

We've all made different discoveries as we've matured. Those discoveries have educated, grown, and developed us. If you want to grow in your spiritual walk with the Lord, be willing to make discoveries.

What are we discovering you may ask? People. That's right, people. For us to change the world, it will require a conscious effort to see the people who are looking for answers. I know you might be saying, "I don't know enough." The only problem with that thought is unless you have an outlet to learn you will never develop new thoughts or exercise the ones you already have. If we as believers don't take the time to discover people, then we are keeping the gift God has given us hidden. For far too long believers have had the "watch my lifestyle approach" which isn't the most effective way to communicate the truth of Christ. We have to do more than have great actions; we must have great interaction as well.

Did Jesus walk around quietly not saying anything, hoping people would see His actions and then believe? No. In fact, most people judged His actions because He did things differently. We've got to get back to discovering people. That means communicating boldly and becoming a friend of sinners, without a fear of being worldly. Who are your friends? Co-workers? Teammates? The people around you are your assignment.

just a trip to Walmart

It was Thanksgiving Day 2009 at Christian Ministries Church in Hot Springs, Arkansas. They were having their annual Thanksgiving meal for anyone in the community who was lonely or hungry. A few days earlier, I was at Walmart getting some items for my wife. A young girl was at the register. Her face was downcast and she looked very frustrated. So my son and I started a conversation with her. We made small talk and then I asked her, "Are you excited about Thanksgiving?" She responded, "No! There is nothing to be excited about. I have to work. I don't get to see my husband. And all of my family is getting together without me. I probably won't even get any turkey."

This conversation broke my heart on many levels, but I was determined to act. You see, I had discovered a need. Right there in Wally World, God gave me an assignment. And for the next few days this girl was on my mind. So when Thanksgiving came, my son, his cousin and I went to Walmart looking for the checkout girl. In our hands were two big take-home boxes of Thanksgiving goodies: turkey, ham, all the fixings, and of course, dessert. We looked everywhere for her and couldn't find her. I had forgotten her name, so I went up to the manager and described this girl. She knew exactly who I was talking about and said, "She is on break. I'll go back and get her." She came out not knowing what to expect. I bet she thought I was some disgruntled shopper. As she came out, I said to her, "I don't know if you remember me. The other day I came in and you were telling me how you weren't looking forward to Thanksgiving." She remembered and nodded her head. Then I said, "I want you to know God loves you very much and I wanted to bring you Thanksgiving dinner. We all have something to be thankful about. I'm giving you this because of the love God has put in my heart." She started bawling. The manager and a few employees started crying as well. She said, "This is the nicest thing that has ever happened to me."

The reason I tell you this story is not to puff myself up. It's so that you can get a vision of the importance of discovering people. The hurting and the lost need friends. We can be that for them. This week, make it a goal to open your eyes and discover people.

tips on how to discover

Notice- It's imperative that we open our eyes to see where we can make a difference. Today, look and listen to those around you and really focus on seeing people. Observe their emotions, passions, problems, and achievements. That will open the door for you to give a hand, some advice, and listen to their stories. Most people are just looking for someone to notice them.

Engage- You won't discover people if you don't communicate with courage and clarity. The fear of failure will keep you from discovering others. To engage in a conversation with someone, just be natural. The point is to show them you are interested. Engaging people is more than just the act of connecting, it's the possibility of a life transformed. To engage may seem hard, but you can do it. Don't allow selfishness to rob you of a victory. Put forth the effort to build a connection that people can trust.

Befriend- Don't be a disciple hunter who is only interested in numbers, but be a friend finder who actually cares about others. Remember you're always looking for someone to invest in. Unless you start a friendship, you will never make it into their social circle. As Christians, we can't stay away from sinners totally. **If we never have time for the lost, how will they be found?** We don't have to agree, promote, or contribute to sin to be a friend. Go to a game, a play, or a concert and start being a legitimate friend.

2. Develop

A real commitment is lived out by the willingness to give instruction and teach others how to get victory. With my children I can discover a problem, but that is not enough. I must develop, teach, and train them or the problem will continue.

Development is an essential part of changing the moral fabric of our nation and the world. But the problem is that development takes committed believers. In order to give wisdom and insight, we must first possess understanding. Gaining understanding doesn't come easy - it requires work, listening, and learning. You can only give what you have! It's the application of personal time in prayer and reading the Bible that will enable you to have something to give. I see many believers with their spiritual tanks empty and they act as though it doesn't matter. Our culture is morally hurting because believers have forfeited their influence. We got busy, started multi-tasking, forgot the scriptures, and became a society of individuals. Here's a sobering statement for you: **if you don't have time for His people, then I can say with all certainty, you're not making time for Him.** People matter!

Jesus and His crew

Jesus understood the principle of development. He didn't have an all-star team already put together. It wasn't like God went and called Moses, David, Joshua, Elisha, and Noah back to the earth to help His boy out. Jesus went and assembled a team of ordinary men who were hungry for something different, something more. If the Son of God had to assemble His team, why wouldn't we? Your team is out there waiting for you to *be the one* who will take the time and care. Right now, they are untrained; it will take patience and a huge commitment from you to be purposeful with your instruction. Sometimes, investing into someone's life gets messy and many of us don't like getting messy.

Jesus dealt with the disciples fighting each other, not wanting to follow, having no faith and not wanting to pray…but His patience prevailed. He took the time to give them the proper mentoring. Nothing will frustrate you more than going through the maturing process with people you mentor. But this is the cycle God has called us to.

Jesus knew that for God's message of grace to be heard, the disciples would have to receive the same revelation He had. We start out as spiritual babies and just like in the physical, we should mature and produce spiritual sons and daughters that go on to cover more ground. We shouldn't be believers who are in a constant stage of nurturing. You see, babies are takers; they give nothing. They care only about comfort and their demands. It's only when you mature that you start to understand giving and considering other people.

However, there is a reason we don't develop: it's because we've bought into the lie that says, "we have nothing to give." I'm writing this to say "yes, you do have something to give." There is something great in you. It was put there before the foundation of the earth. You were made to *be the one.*

tips on how to develop

Invest- The bottom line is that developing takes time and you have to be able to impart something that others want. The apostle Paul said it best when he said, "follow me as I follow Christ".[3] This wasn't a prideful statement; he was simply communicating. "The way I live my life can be modeled." A helpful hint when starting to develop others is that you should first start with people who are not your peers. If you're an older teenager, get involved in your church's junior high ministry. If you're in college, spend some time with high school students. If you're a parent, start looking for young married couples that you can share your experiences with. For people to receive from you they need to see that what you have is valuable.

Equip- Don't be afraid to teach what you know. Everyone knows something. Your goal should be to help the one you're developing avoid the mistakes you made. As you enter into this level of relationship, you become a person of influence in their lives. You become someone to help navigate them through life's tough decisions. Don't take this lightly! This is where accountability, transparency, and connection takes place.

Encourage- Be their biggest fan. Find the areas that they are growing in and bring attention to those areas. Many times it's impossible for an individual to measure their own growth, because they are consumed with all the undeveloped areas. We can open their eyes to see the incredible transformation that is already occurring when we build up.

3. Deploy

Deploying is where we start to take ground for the Lord. This is where all your time and effort pay off. At this stage real change begins because we are producing more believers who are ready to take flight. Just like in the natural process of a bird's development, there will come a point in time when flying is required. For the young bird, the nest is a safe haven where responsibility is limited and growth takes place. This is due to the nourishment of someone else. But make no mistake about it, if the young bird doesn't make the transition from nest to sky then it will never fulfill its call to fly. To stay in the nest would produce dependency or even worse, resentment. This is why it is imperative that we commit to the full process of development and unleash believers to ultimately move out of their spiritual nests.

I've seen too many believers stuck in the nest. The longer young believers stay in the nest the more they become takers. They must launch out and create their own nest. Only then will they continue the reproduction they've been created for.

Our goal is to encourage confident and capable producers who understand the real commitment. This can't happen by producing insecurity in the people we develop. We must allow them to try, fail, and then achieve flight. I implore you to complete the discipleship process in those you mentor by giving them everything they need. This could be the generation of more than just one person making a difference; I'm believing for a community of committed believers poised and ready to *be the one*.

the power of multiplication

How important is just one person who has made the commitment to discover, develop, and deploy? Extremely important! Because one can produce another and this process will continue. This is how we change the world. We must concentrate on deploying active believers who are ready to see a great move of God.

Listen. It's time to get on the same page. It seems like we have become more wrapped up in social issues than issues of the heart. If we are serious about making a difference we must stop fighting individual issues. Let's give attention to the areas that will make the greatest impact. If we start deploying people who have allowed the transformation of the Holy Spirit to take place, then it will just be a matter of time.

Deuteronomy 32:30 says, "one can put a thousand to flight, but two, ten thousand..."[4] This is the beauty of deploying. We do more to spread His message by coming into agreement than by fighting over doctrine. Just think about the revival that would sweep our nation if each believer agreed to reach one person.

Jesus not only gave His disciples wisdom on how to continue the work, He gave them the tools to go out and reproduce what they had experienced. His message became their message. His anthem was their anthem. His work was their work. The benefit of multiplication is that one can influence the masses.

tips on how to deploy

Send- After pouring into a life, understand that the process is not complete until they can reproduce what has been invested in them. Start putting them in situations to communicate what is inside them. Jesus' concept of discipleship was temporarily in, vocationally out. Meaning, He didn't demand that they just stay students. Their focus was to be consumed with sharing the message. To make a difference, start sending people out who are equipped and ready.

Trust- Don't worry about every little thing they do or say. We are not looking for perfection; we are looking for willingness. As you deploy, it's vital that you produce the confidence needed for them to have success. Now that I've been in ministry for many years there are countless truths that I have a deeper understanding in. But if I had never been given the opportunity, then I would not have the influence and wisdom I have today.

Support- As they step into being the one, it's understandable that they will experience many setbacks and disappointments. We are there to help give the right perspective and encourage the work to which God has called them. They need to be reminded that this is not our quest but a work that only God can complete.

david's mark

David left his mark not only as a king but more importantly as a servant of God. We read in psalm after psalm of his transparency with God. And still to this day many have received insight and healing from the words David penned. In fact my favorite psalm by David is Psalm 27:1:

> "The Lord is my light and my salvation; whom shall I fear? The Lord is the refuge of my life; of whom shall I be afraid?"[5]

David changed a nation, restored God's people and loved God. He was the one God ordained to help establish Israel. Now I believe you have been ordained by God to *be the one* to redirect the heart of a lost generation. God has great plans for us. We are not defeated, but the time for action is here!

take the challenge

I challenge you in the next 365 days to find ONE person to mentor! Reading this book will not make you the one just like living in a barn doesn't make you a horse. But, if you will apply these concepts, then, and only then, will you emerge as the one. My prayer is that we start a movement that will change the world.

Go to stevensexton.com/be-the-one and sign up to take the *be the one* challenge. Here, you will be a part of a community of doers who have made the choice to act. With God as our strength there is nothing that is impossible.

Conclusion: Begin The Movement

In spring of 2008, God began to define the message in me to *be the one*. As I was preparing for youth group that night, thought after thought started flooding my heart and mind. It was like a massive download of information that I felt needed to be shared.

My prayer is that this book will begin a movement and spread rapidly so we can see lives spiritually transformed and our nation revitalized. I can't help but think that this is our moment to reclaim what the devil has stolen from us. In order to make a stand, it will require more than well thought out statements. It will require time, attention, and effort.

Many accusations can be made about David, but let me point out that he never lost his kingdom. His kingdom was given to his son and his life ended talking about the greatness of the Lord. Jesus, the son of God, was born through the line of David and in Acts 13 Paul quotes what God said about David's heart.

It is clear that this normal man was used in extraordinary ways. Again, he wasn't chosen because of talent, personality, or intellect. It was his heart that set him apart from other men. His praise, obedience, faith, and commitment provided the access so that God could use him.

use your voice

Regardless of how long you've been in church, the message in this book should focus your attention on the real objective. We must get God's message to the people of this generation. It's imperative that we live, share, invest, equip, and respond to God's master plan. If we don't seize the moment, what is the value of our voice?

I believe the greatest days of the church are ahead. But just as the beauty of a flower garden can fade away because of the amount of weeds that have invaded the area, so can our churches be invaded with the weeds of compromise and ineffectiveness. Our job is to remove the weeds and allow the beauty of God's love to captivate the attention of the lost.

You have a voice in this generation. God has a great plan for you. Don't think it a strange thing that God would choose you to help start a movement. This movement is not a call to arms, or a rebellion against our government. This movement is a call to action. No more silent voices that keep their faith private. The vision is to change the world, but this can only happen if you make the decision to *be the one*. You are not alone. Many have made the commitment to make a difference for Christ. In fact, in his book Tally Ho, The Fox, Herb Hodges wrote:

"One man awake, can waken another;
The second can waken, his next-door brother.
The three awake, can rouse a town,
By turning the whole place upside down,
The many awake, can make such a fuss
That it finally awakens the rest of us.
One man up, with dawn in his eyes, ***multiplies***!"[1]

We are many! And God is ready to do a great work. He is just looking for a willing heart. Start today by joining the *be the one* movement! Go to **stevensexton.com/be-the-one**. Let's get connected and focused on bringing the answer to this generation. Our time is now. Our call is to make a difference! Our moment has come to *be the one*! Let me pray for you:

God, I thank you for the life that is holding this book. I know you have orchestrated their steps and are going to use them mightily in this generation. I'm asking you to pour out your anointing on this believer. Thank you for choosing them to *be the one* to bring your message of truth to their school, family, church, and city. Right now I thank you Lord that they are ready for action and anointed for service. In Jesus' name, Amen.

Acknowledgements

I would like to thank you Lord for entrusting me with this message. To You be all the glory and honor forever!

Unity in the body of Christ is so important. Writing this book has shown me that we need people to accomplish the work that God has given us to do. I would like to thank: Casey Paxton, Greg Hawks, Bob Liggett, Allan Walker, Kevin Rawls, Byron Acosta, Shawn Conrad, Leah Ritthaler, Jessica Wells, Marie Olson, Verlie Lamb, Rachel Wood and Adam Jones for helping make this book the best that it can be.

Also I'd like to thank all the leaders and mentors who've helped me *be the one*. My deepest thanks to my mom, Bonny Sexton, and also to Don and Hettie Lue Brooks, Tim and Terri Brooks, Paul and Angela Kern, Lloyd Withrow, Rueban Morales, Keith Ashcrath, Bob Simonette, and Dr. Jaffus Hardrick—all of your marks on my life have enabled me to know the Lord on a greater level.

To my wife Katie who was my primary proof reader and encourager. Love ya Babe! Thank you so much.

End Notes

Chapter 1

1. 1 Samuel 15:27-28
2. Luke 10:2
3. Matthew 28:19-20, paraphrased
4. Ezekiel 22:30
5. Romans 8:31
6. The International Journal of Not for Profit Law volume 9, issue 1
7. 1 Peter 1:12 paraphrased
8. Esther 4:12-14

Chapter 2

1. 1 Samuel 16:7
2. Psalm 139:14
3. Luke 1:31
4. Luke 1:30
5. Luke 1:38
6. Numbers 13:31, paraphrased
7. Hebrews 11:6
8. John 14:15
9. Psalm 75:6, KJV
10. Proverbs 3:34, NKJV
11. Romans 8:31

Chapter 3

1. 1 Samuel 16:17-19
2. Psalm 37:4
3. 1 Samuel 16:17-19

4. Charlie and the Chocolate Factory. Tim Burton. Johnny Depp, Freddie Highmore. Warner Brothers, 15 July 2005.
5. I Corinthians 10:13, Paraphrased
6. Matt 25:14-30, paraphrased

Chapter 4

1. II Corinthians 10:5
2. Romans 8:31
3. Exodus 14:14
4. Psalm 139:2
5. Ephesians 6:12, paraphrased
6. John 6:44, paraphrased
7. Matthew 5:45, paraphrased
8. 1 Samuel 17:26, paraphrased
9. Hebrews 11:6

Chapter 5

1. Genesis 3 and Matthew 4
2. Exodus 4
3. Romans 13: 1-4
4. Matthew 25:23
5. Colossians 3:18-21
6. Ephesians 6:1-4
7. Ephesians 6:5-9
8. Hebrews 13:17
9. Romans 13:1-7
10. Galatians 6:7
11. 1 Samuel 26:7-11

Chapter 6

1. 2 Samuel 11:1-5, paraphrased
2. 2 Samuel 11:12- 24
3. Mark 4:22 NKJV

4. Hebrews 12:2 NKJV
5. Luke 19:17 NKJV
6. 2 Corinthians 12:10 NKJV
7. James 1:17, paraphrased
8. Hebrews 13:8
9. Mark 6:32-34
10. Romans 3:23
11. 2 Samuel 12:13
12. Revelation 3:19

Chapter 7

1. Acts 13:22
2. 1 Kings 2:3
3. James 1:12 NKJV
4. John 6:50-69

Chapter 8

1. McKay Hatch. No Cussing Club. 2010. July 2, 2010. http://www.nocussing.com/aboutncc.html.
2. Tracy Rysavy. Free the Children: The Story of Craig Kielburger. September 30, 1999. July 2, 2010. http://www.yesmagazine.org/issues/power-of-one/free-the-children-the-story-of-craig-kielburger.
3. 1 Corinthians 11:1, paraphrased
4. Deuteronomy 32:30 NKJV
5. Psalm 27:1

Conclusion

1. Hodges, Herb. Tally Ho, The Fox: The Foundation for building world-visionary, world impacting, reproducing disciples. Bloomington, Minnesota: Bethany House Publishers, 1985. Print.

CPSIA information can be obtained at www.ICGtesting.com
Printed in the USA
LVOW030717031111

253323LV00002B/3/P